CUPS Administrative Guide

A practical tutorial to installing, managing, and securing this powerful printing system

Ankur Shah

PUBLISHING

BIRMINGHAM - MUMBAI

CUPS Administrative Guide

First published: September 2008

Production Reference: 1190908

Published by Packt Publishing Ltd.
32 Lincoln Road
Olton
Birmingham, B27 6PA, UK.

ISBN 978-1-84719-258-5

www.packtpub.com

Cover Image by Vinayak Chittar (vinayak.chittar@gmail.com)

Credits

Author

Ankur Shah

Reviewer

Aric Pedersen

Acquisition Editor

Rashmi Phadnis

Technical Editor

Gagandeep Singh

Copy Editor

Sumathi Sridhar

Editorial Team Leader

Akshara Aware

Project Manager

Abhijeet Deobhakta

Project Coordinator

Lata Basantani

Indexer

Monica Ajmera

Proofreaders

Claire Lane

Chris Smith

Production Coordinator

Shantanu Zagade

Cover Work

Shantanu Zagade

About the Author

Ankur Shah has been working with Linux/AIX for the last four years as a System Administrator. His previous assignment was with Packt Publishing, where he worked as System Administrator and also started implementing CUPS. He completed his graduation in Computer Engineering from Nagpur University, India. He is currently working as a SAP Basis Administrator and also started working on Governance Risk and Compliance for access Control. He is also interested in Oracle Database Administration and Security.

He is the biggest fan of Kajol. The day her movie releases is a day of celebration for him and he only parties once a year—5th August—that's Kajol's birthday. It goes without saying that he watches all her movies several times—often dragging his friends and family to participate in his madness.

Acknowledgement

Mummy, Papa, and Nani – thanks for your love and support. Even though I am not with you all the time, you are always there in my heart.

I would like to thank Vicky, Dhruti, Sunilkumar, Harde, Vevayji, Vevanji, Rakeshbhai, Ravibhai, and Buntybhai.

I would like to remember Bipinkaka who passed away this year. He was someone I admired a lot.

Thanks to Sarojkaki, Ujwal, Leniya, Amitkumar, Binita, Priteshkumar, Moksha, Motapapa, Motimummy, Mamtaben, Nilesh Jiju, Kalpeshbhai, Reenabhabhi , Hirenbhai , Bhavibhabhi, Akasha, Sagar, Urvi, Babulafuva, Pushpafoya, Jayben, Nareshjiju, Dhansukhbhai, Tarabhabhi, Guddi, Mayurkumar, Pintoo, Bablu, Kinjal, Praveenfuva, Hansafoya, Pankajiju, Alpaben, ,Pankaj bhai, Sangeetabhabhi, Leenabe, Manjojiju, Bimalbhai, Komalbhabhi, Kinjal, Chiku, Amar, Jheel, Viral,Krish, Rujul, Kushi, Vidulamasi, Masaji, Ripalbhai, Bhabhi , Chitan, Pinkiben and her family, and all my other relatives not mentioned here due to lack of space.

I would also like to remember all my neighbors and friends: Dr Uncle, Nayna Aunty, Jigar, Trusha, Babu, Gaugang, Rahul, Tinuben and their parents, Kalpesh Sir, Shailesh and his family, Shashikant Sir and his family, Kavitaben and her family.

All my college friends Jignesh, Manish, Sandeep, Parag, Mausam, Prashant, Jaydeep, Jigar, Tapan, Shaunak, Divyesh, Nirav, Pritesh, Deepak, Lokesh.
Thanks also to Aarti , Vushal, Amit, Ajit, Ramesh, Kaiser, Vinod, Kailash, Umesh, Rajendra, Digambar, Sandeep, Arun, Vikat.

A big token of gratitude to Ninad Sir from Interpole Technologies who was the reason I started working on Linux.

Many, many thanks to Dipali—she has always been there to support and guide me.

I can't let this opportunity pass without mentioning my ex-colleagues at Packt – Sandeep, Shelly, Manjiri, Jimmy, Priyanka, Tripti, Shravani, Teerth, Manu and their friends Nikhil da Dawggie and Ved da Prakash Jha, Raj, Bansari, Saurabh, Sagara, Tints, Ritika, Zenab, Aboli, Devdoot Naidu, Girish, and Rajeev (thanks a lot buddy).

Thanks to Packt where I found so many of my friends—Lata, Poochi, Monica, Shantanu, Nilpreet, Patricia, Sumathi, my previous AEs (Nanda, Viraj, and Shayantani), Silpa <3 Sameer, Rameshbhau, Harshada, Neelanchal, Swarna, Ajay, Swapna, Akshara, Mithil, Abhijeet, and Bhushan.

Special thanks to Rupaldee and Mineshjiju (with whom I have been living for the last four years), Dada/Dadi who have treated me like a son, Mudra my niece and Chandra my nephew (two of my favorite chelas), Mayankjiju, Neetaben, Bimaljiju, Chhayaben, Prakashjiju, Nimishaben, Vevayji, Vama, Dhara, Labdhi, Reeti, Mitwa, and Jainam.

Thanks to all my neighbors at Mumbai—Pradeepmasa, Masi, Ruchi, Snehalbhai, Masa-Masi, Nehadidi, Pradeepbhaiya, Niyatididi, Heet, Anushka, and Bhavya.

Louay Fatoohi—for believing in me and giving me the opportunity to work on this book.

Special thanks to Rashmi—she always believed in me and without her this book would never have been completed.

And finally the real architect of this book, Aric Pedersen. VPJ was right when he said, *Author book thode hi na banata hai, reviewer banata hai.* Aric is everything that the open source culture stands for. He is a great guy to work with and I wish the world is overrun with his clones.

About the Reviewer

Aric Pedersen is the author of *cPanel User Guide and Tutorial* (978-1-904811-92-3) and *Web Host Manager Administration Guide* (978-1-904811-50-3) both written for Packt Publications. He has over 8 years experience serving as a systems administrator. He also works for Netenberg.com, creators of Fantastico, the first and most popular web script autoinstaller for cPanel servers.

Kajol, this book is dedicated to you.
You have always been my inspiration since the day I watched DDLJ for the first time.
I know you like reading books and this is the only one I could write.

Table of Contents

Preface

The Common UNIX Printing System (CUPS) that is provided under the GNU General Public License (GPL) and GNU Library General Public License (LGPL), Version 2, allows you to print from applications such as the web browser. CUPS uses the Internet Printing Protocol (IPP) for managing print jobs, print queues, and it adds network printer browsing and PostScript Printer Description-based printing options. CUPS was first developed by Easy Software Products, but it is currently owned and maintained by Apple Inc.

CUPS converts the page descriptions produced by your application (put a paragraph here, draw a line there, and so forth) into something your printer can understand, and then sends the information to the printer for printing.

Now, since every printer manufacturer does things differently, printing can be very complicated. CUPS does its best to hide this from you and your application so that you can concentrate more on printing and less on how to print. Generally, the only time you need to know anything about your printer is when you use it for the first time, and even then, CUPS can often figure things out on its own.

What This Book Covers

Chapter 1 covers the history of UNIX printing systems which includes traditional printing systems such as Berkeley printing system and System V printing System. We will also cover how CUPS evolves as a printing system, along with the architecture of CUPS.

Chapter 2 checks the pre-requisites for downloading and installing CUPS software. It also includes restarting CUPS service and accessing it via web interface.

Chapter 3 discusses the printer drivers that CUPS supports. We will also see how to manage printers and jobs using the Command-Line Tool (`lpadmin`) and the Web GUI Interface. This will include how to add, modify, delete, stop, and share printers, setting up options on printers, and how to cancel, move, restart jobs, and so on.

Chapter 4 looks at how to group multiple printers (printer classes), and how to manage them using the command-line tool and the web interface as in the previous chapter.

Chapter 5 covers the topic of system requirements for a CUPS print server. This chapter mainly discusses the server configuration file `cupsd.conf` and its directives, and the configuration files for printers (`printers.conf`), and classes (`classes.conf`).

Chapter 6 looks at setting up a client on various platforms such as UNIX/Linux, Windows, and Mac OS X using protocols such as LPD (Line Printer Demon), IPP (Internet Printing Protocol), and SMB (Server Message Block). It also has a section on how to use printer setups along with other printing systems.

Chapter 7 covers how we set up quotas on all CUPS users using the command-line tool, and an overview of the `page_log` file. This chapter also covers other accounting tools that can work with CUPS. Here, we discuss PyKota in detail.

Chapter 8 looks at monitoring CUPS using the `lpstat` command, and has an overview of the `access_log` and the `error_log` files. We will also see how Simple Network Management Protocol (SNMP) helps CUPS discover the printer and help other networking tools such as Cacti in managing printers.

Chapter 9 covers an overview of how CUPS recognizes different file formats with the help of the `mime.types` file. This chapter also covers how CUPS uses various filters to convert one file format into another specified in the `mime.convs` file.

Chapter 10 looks at how TCP/IP printers can be managed. This will also cover the support of encryption and various authentication methods such as basic, digest, and Kerberos. This chapter will also cover the topic on a possible Denial of Service (DoS) that can occur in CUPS.

What You Need for This Book

To get the most from this book you will need a copy of the CUPS server software and one or more PCs on which to install it. You will need the ability to run UNIX/Linux commands to install the software. You will need a printer with drivers for that printer.

Printers in CUPS can be managed either via a command line or a web interface. This web interface can work on almost any web browser including Firefox, Safari, or the Internet Explorer. Here it is assumed that the reader has a basic knowledge of using the browser software. Since CUPS can also work across a local network/the Internet, you will need a network/Internet and a separate client PC, if you want to use this feature.

Conventions

In this book, you will find a number of styles of text that distinguish between different kinds of information. Here are some examples of these styles, and an explanation of their meaning.

Code words in text are shown as follows: "We can include other contexts through the use of the `include` directive."

A block of code will be set as follows:

```
<interfaces>
    <lan>
        <ipaddr>192.168.1.251</ipaddr>
        <subnet>24</subnet>
        <gateway>192.168.1.254</gateway>
```

Any command-line input and output is written as follows:

```
Apr 1 11:06:00        kernel: real memory = 268435456 (256 MB)
Apr 1 11:06:00        kernel: avail memory = 252907520 (241 MB)
```

New terms and **important words** are introduced in a bold-type font. Words that you see on the screen, in menus or dialog boxes for example, appear in our text like this: "clicking the **Next** button moves you to the next screen".

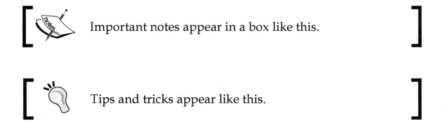

Important notes appear in a box like this.

Tips and tricks appear like this.

Reader Feedback

Feedback from our readers is always welcome. Let us know what you think about this book, what you liked or may have disliked. Reader feedback is important for us to develop titles that you really get the most out of.

To send us general feedback, simply drop an email to feedback@packtpub.com, making sure to mention the book title in the subject of your message.

If there is a book that you need and would like to see us publish, please send us a note in the **SUGGEST A TITLE** form on www.packtpub.com or email suggest@packtpub.com.

If there is a topic that you have expertise in and you are interested in either writing or contributing to a book, see our author guide on www.packtpub.com/authors.

Customer Support

Now that you are the proud owner of a Packt book, we have a number of things to help you to get the most from your purchase.

Errata

Although we have taken every care to ensure the accuracy of our contents, mistakes do happen. If you find a mistake in one of our books—maybe a mistake in text or code—we would be grateful if you would report this to us. By doing this you can save other readers from frustration, and help to improve subsequent versions of this book. If you find any errata, report them by visiting http://www.packtpub.com/support, selecting your book, clicking on the **let us know** link, and entering the details of your errata. Once your errata are verified, your submission will be accepted and the errata added to the list of existing errata. The existing errata can be viewed by selecting your title from http://www.packtpub.com/support.

Piracy

Piracy of copyright material on the Internet is an ongoing problem across all media. At Packt, we take the protection of our copyright and licenses very seriously. If you come across any illegal copies of our works in any form on the Internet, please provide the location address or website name immediately so we can pursue a remedy.

Please contact us at copyright@packtpub.com with a link to the suspected pirated material.

We appreciate your help in protecting our authors, and our ability to bring you valuable content.

Questions

You can contact us at `questions@packtpub.com` if you are having a problem with some aspect of the book, and we will do our best to address it.

1
Introduction

CUPS is the abbreviation for Common UNIX Printing System. It is a modularized computer printing system for UNIX-like operating systems, which provides a common printing interface across a local network, masking differences among the printing systems on each computer. A computer running CUPS is a host that can accept print jobs from client computers, process them, and send them to the appropriate printer. It was developed by Easy Software Products **(ESP)** and is now owned and maintained by Apple Inc. Now CUPS is the standard printing system in most Linux distributions.

 Common UNIX Printing System (CUPS) is the base for streamlined printing systems for Mac OS X. CUPS can also work independently on Mac OS X. You can get more information on this at:

http://developer.apple.com/printing/overview.html

In this chapter, we will discuss the various features of CUPS, and the support of PostScript Printer Driver (PPD) in detail.

Overview of the CUPS Features

CUPS consists of a print spooler and a scheduler, a filter system that converts the print data to a format that the printer will understand, and a backend system that sends this data to the print device.

CUPS uses the Internet Printing Protocol (IPP) to manage print jobs and queues. It also provides the traditional System V and Berkeley command line interfaces. It also provides limited support for the Server Message Block (SMB) protocol. The device drivers supplied by CUPS are based on PostScript Printer Description (PPD) files. There are a number of user interfaces for different computing platforms that can configure CUPS, and it has a built-in, web-based interface.

History of Printing in UNIX

In the early versions of UNIX, the line printer daemon (LPD) was used to spool text to a printer. This LPD also known as Berkeley printing system (BSD) is able to send any kind of file to a printer.

The model of this printing system consists of the following features:

- A number of hosts request print services from a LPD process running on a host
- The output of the print job will be produced when a file is sent as a request input
- The print job will have a unique number from 0 to 999
- Users who request print jobs shouldn't have their user name starting with digits
- Apart from its main command lpd, the system also supports lpr (assign to queue), lpq (display the queue), lprm (remove from queue), and lpc (control the queue)

The biggest disadvantage with the Berkeley printing system is that it doesn't provide any feature for print jobs and filtering systems. These features were added in a new line printer (LP) system. The following URL shows information about this system in detail:

`http://tools.ietf.org/html/rfc1179`

 A printer that supports LPD/LPR is sometimes referred to as a "TCP/IP printer". The LPD/LPR protocol listens on TCP port 515.

The System V printing system is one of the several standard architectures for printing on the UNIX platform which uses the lp command. The following are some of the features of System V printing system:

- This printing system is applicable to commercial System V based OS such as Solaris SCO OpenServer
- Solaris has done a lot of modifications due to its open source project *OpenSolaris* by keeping original System V printing system intact

OpenSolaris is an open source project created by Sun Microsystems to build a developer community around Solaris Operating System technology. You can get more information on this at:
`http://opensolaris.org/os/`

- Apart from its main command `lp`, System V uses other commands such as `lpstat` (shows the current print queue), `cancel` (deletes a job from the print queue), `lpadmin` (an administrative command to configure the print system), `lpmove` (an administrative command to configure moves jobs between queues)

CUPS emulates both System V and Berkeley print architectures at the interface level, though its internal architecture is different from both. We will see the architecture of CUPS with its features shortly.

Printing with Personal Computers

Early personal computers, such as the ones from IBM, and printers only handled text. So they worked in a fashion similar to the UNIX mainframes of that time. Each application came with its own code to handle text-based printing to popular printers. Most of those applications are shipped with modules that help users print to their specific printers.

As the technology improved, printers began to support graphics, so applications had to adapt support the expanded printer features. The complexity of the software used to communicate with printers soon began to rival the applications themselves, and it wasn't long before that these "printer drivers" were an industry of their own. Unfortunately, a printer driver for one application rarely worked with another, so the applications had to adapt support the expanded printer features.

Apple's release of the *Macintosh* computer changed the manner in which printing was done on the personal computer. Designed from the beginning to be a desktop publishing system, the Macintosh abstracted the printing interface from the application. Applications only had to tell the printing system where and what to print, and the printing system would translate that request into the desired output on the selected printer. Printer drivers were provided with the Mac OS or with the printer you purchased for your computer. The same driver supported all Mac OS applications. Arguably, the Mac OS has dominated desktop publishing since its inception. To this day, a large number of printing shops use the Mac OS for their work.

Microsoft's first Windows operating environment duplicated this paradigm. The printing and information display systems are nothing alike, technically. However, to an end user, they seem to work similarly. Applications for these operating systems were able to produce professional-quality output with a generic printing interface. Yet until recently, UNIX only had a print file spooling system.

Evolution of CUPS as a Printing System

In 1993, a company called Easy Software Products (ESP) was started, aimed at supporting the Digital UNIX and Linux operating systems. Unfortunately, these operating systems used the original LPD for printing, so you couldn't pass options to the printer drivers. This alone would cripple any drivers you could develop. To make matters more complicated, at least three versions of the LPD were in common use, and they were not 100% compatible with each other.

The original design of the Common UNIX Printing System (CUPS) was based around the LPD network protocol. Later, developers added support for various features such as remote administration, and authentication when the Internet Printing Protocol (IPP) working group was created. The IPP working group originally was just going to update the LPD network protocol, but quickly changed direction to create a much more functional and extensible protocol that could evolve as needed to support new technologies.

Architecture of CUPS

CUPS provides a mechanism that allows print jobs to be sent to printers in a standard fashion. The data is sent to a scheduler, which then sends jobs to a filter system that converts the print job into a format which the printer will understand. The filter system then passes the data on to a **backend** — a special filter that sends print data to a device or a network connection.

The primary advantage of CUPS is that it is a standard and modularized printing system that can process numerous data formats on the print server. Previously, it was difficult to find a standardized solution that would allow numerous printers to print their full feature sets. For instance, the System V and Berkeley printing systems were largely incompatible with each other, and they required setting up complicated scripts and workarounds to convert from the program's data format to a format the printer understood. They often didn't know how to detect the file format that was being sent to the printer and thus could not convert data correctly. They also did their data conversion on the workstation and not on the server.

With CUPS, it is far easier for printer manufacturers and printer driver developers to create drivers that work natively on the print server than before. As the processing is done on the server, it is also easier to allow for network-based printing. Another advantage that CUPS has is that when it is used with Samba software, the printers can be used for remote print from and to Windows PCs.

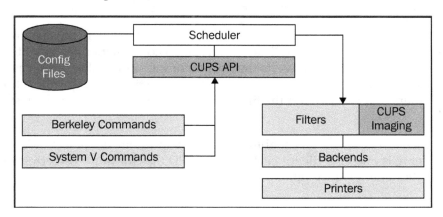

Scheduler

The scheduler is a HTTP/1.1 server application that handles HTTP requests. Besides handling printer requests via IPP POST requests, the scheduler also acts as a full-featured web server for documentation, status monitoring, and administration. The scheduler also manages a list of available printers on the LAN and dispatches print jobs as needed using the appropriate filters and backends.

Configuration Files

The configuration files consist of:

- The HTTP server configuration file
- Printer and class definition files
- MIME type and conversion rule files
- PostScript Printer Description (PPD) files

The HTTP server configuration file is purposely similar to the Apache web server configuration file and defines all the access control properties for the server.

The printer and class definition files list the available printer queues and classes. Printer classes are collections of printers. Jobs sent to a class are forwarded to the first available printer in the class, in a round-robin fashion.

The MIME type files list the supported MIME (Multipurpose Internet Mail Extensions) types (text/plain, application/postscript, and so on) and the "magic" rules for automatically detecting the format of a file. These are used by the HTTP server to determine the Content-Type field for GET and HEAD requests and by the IPP request handler to determine the file type when a Print-Job or Send-File request is received with a document format of `application/octet-stream`.

The MIME conversion rule files list the available filters. The filters are used when a job is dispatched, so that an application can send a convenient file format to the printing system which then converts the document into a printable format as needed. Each filter has a relative cost associated with it, and the filtering algorithm chooses the set of filters that will convert the file to the needed format with the lowest total "cost".

The PPD files can describe the capabilities of all the printers, not just PostScript printers. There is one PPD file for each printer. PPD files for non-PostScript printers define additional filters through CUPS Filter attributes to support printer drivers.

CUPS API

The CUPS API contains CUPS-specific convenience functions for queuing print jobs, getting printer information, accessing resources via HTTP and IPP, and manipulating PPD files. Unlike the rest of CUPS, the CUPS API is provided under the terms of the GNU LGPL, so it may be used by non-GPL applications.

 You can get detailed information on the license of CUPS and other supported software at:
`http://www.cups.org/documentation.php/license.html`

Berkeley and System V Commands

CUPS provides the System V and Berkeley command-line interfaces for submitting jobs and checking the printer status. The `lpstat` and `lpc` status commands also show network printers ("printer server") when printer browsing is enabled.

The System V administration commands are supplied for managing printers and classes. The Berkeley printer administration tool (`lpc`) is only supported in a "read-only" mode to check the current status of the printer queues and the scheduler.

Filters

A filter program reads from the standard input or from a file if a filename is supplied, and then sends the output to the backend in a format the printer recognizes. The filters supports a common set of options including printer name, job ID, username, job title, number of copies, and job options. Filters are provided for many file formats and include image file and PostScript raster filters that support non–PostScript printers. Multiple filters are run in parallel to produce the required output format.

The PostScript raster filter is based on the GNU Ghostscript. Instead of using the Ghostscript printer drivers and frontend, the CUPS filter uses a generic raster printer driver and CUPS-compliant frontend to support any kind of raster printer. This allows the same printer driver filter to be used for printing raster data from any filter. We will discuss all CUPS based drivers such as PostScript Printer Drivers (PPD), Ghostscript drivers and so on in detail in the section, *Printer Drivers* in Chapter 3 on *Printer Management*.

CUPS Imaging

The CUPS Imaging library provides functions for managing large images, doing colorspace conversion and color management, scaling images for printing, and managing raster page streams. It is used by the CUPS image file filters, the PostScript RIP, and all raster printer drivers.

> PostScript Raster Image Processors (RIP) are the filters that convert PostScript files into high resolution raster images. This means that the RIP can take the digital information about fonts and graphics that describe the appearance of your file and translate it into an image composed of individual dots that the imaging device.

Backends

A backend program is a special filter that sends print data to a device or network connection. This program is usually located in /usr/lib/cups/backend/. The backends for parallel, serial, usb, lpd, ipp, and socket (for AppSocket & JetDirect) connections are provided in CUPS 1.1 & the later versions. The SAMBA version 2.0.6 and higher includes a SMB backend (smbspool) that can be used with CUPS 1.0 or higher for printing to Windows.

Network Printing

Traditionally, network printing has been one of the hardest things to get working under UNIX. One reason is that each vendor added his or her own extensions to the LPD protocol (the previous standard for network printing), making cross-platform printing difficult, if not impossible.

Another reason is that you have to administer each network printer on each client machine. In some cases, you can "clone" the printer configuration from a "master" client to each of the others, but even that can be time consuming and error-prone. Something better is needed.

CUPS provides **printer browsing**, which allows clients to automatically see and use printers from any server on a LAN. This means that you only need to configure the server, and the clients will automatically see the printers and classes on it. The feature will be discussed in Chapter 8 — *Monitoring CUPS* where we explore SNMP protocol within CUPS.

In addition, CUPS can automatically merge multiple identical network printers into "implicit classes". This allows clients to send jobs to the implicit class and have them print on the first available printer. In addition, failsafe and load-balancing functions are enabled simply by defining the same printer on multiple servers. The feature of classes will be discussed in Chapter 4 — *Managing Multiple Printers at a Time*.

CUPS Features

The following are the features of CUPS. We will discuss each of this features in detail:

- Support for Internet Printing Protocol (IPP)
- Compatibility with other Print Systems
- Support for Web Interface
- Modular Architecture
- Support For PostScript Printer Description Drivers (PPDs)

Support for Internet Printing Protocol (IPP)

IPP is a protocol for an industry and Internet Engineering Task Force (IETF) standard that supports network printing. CUPS supports the Internet Printing Protocol (IPP) that is supported under all UNIX/Linux platforms, and also under Novell's Netware and recent Windows OS. Since it is widely supported and well-documented, IPP alone comes close to solving one of the biggest administration nightmares on most networks, cross-platform printing. Some higher end network printers now support IPP too. In addition to supporting sending and receiving print jobs, the IPP protocol also supports features such as browsing. Browsing allows the automatic configuration of printers on a network. An IPP host may broadcast information about its printer list to a particular network. The other IPP hosts on the network may then add this printer information to their printer list. This allows the administrator to add the printer to one host and have the new printer appear as an option on all of the desktop PCs in the organization.

Since IPP is destined to work across all operating system platforms, you can create **unified** sets of query functions that can be used on IPP-enabled printers and servers for transferring files, and setting job-control attributes among others. However, rollout of IPP will not happen overnight, as many legacy print devices will still be in use for many years to come. To overcome this, IPP has a provision for backward compatibility of all IPP implementations including CUPS.

The most striking advantage of IPP is its integration into the existing set of other robust IP protocols. Internet Printing Protocol (IPP) being an extension of the proven and robust HTTP 1.1 protocol is also very easy to plug in other standards as they are being developed and deployed for the special task of handling print file and related data. The following are some of the features of IPP. We will discuss each of this in detail later in this book:

- Supports various authentication methods such as basic, digest, Kerberos, and local certificate for users seeking access to print services
- Supports SSL3 and TLS encryption for transferring data. Both these points will be covered in Chapter 10 — *Security*
- Bi-directional communication of clients with print devices, using the HTTP/ IPP **GET** and **POST** mechanism
- LDAP (Lightweight Directory Address Protocol) directory service integration to keep a consistent database of available printers, their capabilities and page costs, and so on, as well as user passwords, ACL's among others
- **Pull** (as opposed to the usual "Push" model) printing, where a server or printer just needs to be told the URL of a document, whereupon it is retrieved from the resource on the internet and printed

Compatibility with Other Print Systems

The following are the systems that are compatible with CUPS:

- BSD and SysV print systems over network and command-line tools
- Windows print system with the help of Samba
- Socket printing for printing to AppSocket, HP JetDirect, and other similar devices

We will see printer related commands in Chapter 3—*Managing Printers*. In Chapter 6, we will cover CUPS printing with clients working on different platforms. The same chapter will also cover printing with Samba and other systems.

Support for Web Interface

CUPS provides web interface for management. The interface provides various features for printer, classes, and jobs. Since the IPP protocol is very similar to the HTTP protocol, it was quite easy for the CUPS team to write a web-based configuration tool into the CUPS service. The interface also includes options to view important log files, configuration files, authentication, and administration options. You can also configure and maintain a CUPS host's print queues from any machine that has a web browser. CUPS owes lots of to the web interface for its popularity and that's why we will be using various features of CUPS web interface in almost all the chapters in this book.

Modular Architecture

CUPS is designed to be very modular. To add new functionality, such as better accounting or support for a new network print protocol, someone just needs to write a small component that serves the intended purpose and plugs it into the CUPS print system.

Support of Postscript Printer Description Drivers (PPDs) in CUPS

Before we learn about PostScript drivers, let's first understand PostScript.

The PostScript programming language is an invention by Adobe, but its specifications have been published extensively. Its strength lies in its powerful ability to describe graphical objects (fonts, shapes, patterns, lines, curves, and dots), their attributes (color, linewidth), and the way to manipulate (scale, distort, rotate, shift) them. Since it is relatively easier, anybody with the required skill can start writing his or her own implementation of a PostScript interpreter and use it to display PostScript files on screen, or on paper.

PPD (Postscript Printer Description) file is a file that describes the fonts, paper sizes, resolution, and other capabilities that are standard for a particular Postscript printer. PostScript Printer Descriptions Driver (PPDs) is a program that uses these PPD file to understand the capabilities of a particular printer. CUPS not only supports PPD Drivers for all PostScript printer drivers, but also for non-PostScript Printers.

We will discuss PPDs in the section *Printer Drivers* of Chapter 3 and also in Chapter 9 in detail where we shall discuss *Filtering* in detail.

Summary

The Common UNIX Print System (CUPS) has become quite popular. All major Linux distributions now ship it as their default printing system. People tend to regard it as a "black box", and they do not want to look at too closely as long as it works properly. But once there is a problem, they have trouble finding out where to start debugging.

CUPS supports quite a few unique and powerful features. The basic functions of CUPS is relatively quite easy, but since CUPS has various new features such as support of IPP, availability of web interface, a modular architecture, and so on. It is best not to try to apply any prior knowledge about printing to this new system.

CUPS is more than just a print spooling system. It is a complete printer management system that complies with the new Internet Printing Protocol (IPP). Many of its functions can be managed remotely (or locally) or via a web browser (giving you platform-independent access to the CUPS print server). Additionally, it has a traditional command-line and several more modern GUI interfaces, which we shall explore in the forthcoming chapters. In the next chapter, we will discuss how to install and configure CUPS.

2
Building and Installing CUPS

Today, most of the UNIX and Linux systems come with the CUPS printing system. CUPS is supported by Caldera, Debian, Conectiva, easyLinux, HP-UX, IRIX, Linux Mandrake, Peanut, Red Hat, Solaris, SusE, Tru64, UNIX, TurboLinux, and AIX. Of these, Conectiva, easyLinux, Linux Mandrake, and Peanut use CUPS as their primary printing system.

This chapter describes how to compile and install CUPS on your system from the source code.

Downloading Source Code

Today, most of the UNIX and Linux distributions install CUPS by default. CUPS requires ANSI-compliant C and C++ compilers, a Make program and Bourne shell. The GNU compiler tools also work well with CUPS.

CUPS has been tested with GNU Make as well as the other Make programs shipped by Compaq, HP, SGI, and Sun. BSD users should use GNU make (gmake). The latest version of CUPS can be downloaded from `http://www.cups.org/software.php`. The current stable version of CUPS is 1.3.8.

Apart from these tools, we also require support for the following libraries that provides additional functionality for printing service. CUPS mainly supports two libraries:

- CUPS imaging library
- CUPS library

The CUPS imaging library consists of libraries for JPEG, PNG, TIFF, ZLIB, and so on, and it is used for images support.

The CUPS library contains CUPS-specific functions that support the use of CDSA, GNU TLS, and the OpenSSL libraries for encryption. We will discuss these in details in Chapter 10, on *Security*. For the directory service, you can use the OpenLDAP and the OpenSLP libraries.

You can find a mirror of CUPS related libraries which is maintained by Easy Software Products at:

`ftp://ftp.easysw.com/pub/libraries`.

[CUPS can easily compile and run without above libraries. However, you will miss out on many of the features provided by CUPS.]

If any changes need to be made in the man pages, you will need GNU Troff (Groff) or another nroff-like package. Groff is available at `ftp://ftp.gnu.org/gnu/groff/`.

The documentation is formatted using the HTMLDOC software. If you need to make changes, you can get the HTMLDOC software from `http://www.htmldoc.org/index.php`.

Compiling CUPS

The source code of CUPS is available in two formats:

- `Gnu zip` — with `.gz` extension
- `bzip2` — with `.bz2` extension

Once you download the source code for the CUPS, it must be extracted using the following command:

`#tar -xvf cups-1.3.8-source.tar.gz`

Or

`#tar xvjf cups-1.3.8-source.tar.bz2`

In the example above, `cups-1.3.8-source.tar.gz` is the source code of CUPS in a `.gz` format. To compile the source code, we need to go to the CUPS source directory which has just been created.

`#cd cups-1.3.8`

CUPS uses GNU Autoconf to configure the Makefiles and source code for your system. Type the following command to configure CUPS for your system:

`#./configure`

The default installation will put the CUPS software in the /etc, /usr, and /var directories on your system, which will overwrite all existing print commands on your system.

You can also use the --prefix option to install the CUPS software in another location:

```
#./configure --prefix=/some/directory
```

You can see a complete list of configuration options using the --help option:

```
#./configure --help
```

If the PNG, JPEG, TIFF, and ZLIB libraries are not installed in a system in the default location (typically /usr/include and /usr/lib), we need to set the CFLAGS,CPPFLAGS, CXXFLAGS, DSOFLAGS and LDFLAGS environment variables prior to configuration:

```
        setenv CFLAGS "-I/any/dir"
        setenv CPPFLAGS "-I/any/dir"
        setenv CXXFLAGS "-I/any/dir"
        setenv DSOFLAGS "-Lany/dir"
        setenv LDFLAGS "-L/any/dir"
        ./configure
```

Or

```
        CFLAGS="-I/any/dir" \
        CPPFLAGS="-I/any/dir" \
        CXXFLAGS="-I/any/dir" \
        DSOFLAGS="-L/any/dir" \
        LDFLAGS="-L/any/dir" \
        ./configure
```

To enable support for encryption, you will need to add the --enable-ssl option:

```
#./configure --enable-ssl
```

SSL and TLS support requires the OpenSSL library, which is available at http://www.openssl.org.

If the OpenSSL headers and libraries are not installed in the standard directories, you can configure them using --with-openssl-includes and --with-openssl-libs options:

```
 #./configure --enable-ssl \
    --with-openssl-includes=/foo/bar/include \
    --with-openssl-libs=/foo/bar/lib
```

Once the configuration is done, you can start building the software by using the following command:

```
#make
```

If you are using FreeBSD, NetBSD, or OpenBSD systems, use the following command instead:

```
#gmake
```

Installing the Software

Once the CUPS software is built, you need to install it. The `install` target provides a quick way to install the software on your local system:

```
#make install
```

You should use the following command to install built CUPS, if the system is FreeBSD, NetBSD, or OpenBSD:

```
#gmake install
```

> Installing CUPS will overwrite your existing printing system. If you experiences difficulties with the CUPS software and want to go back to your old printing system, the reinstallation of the old printing system can be done via the operating system CDs.

If you find any difficulties with compiling CUPS, you can submit a trouble report on the CUPS website. The Software Trouble Reports (STR) are maintained on the **Bugs and Feature** page on the CUPS website: `http://www.cups.org/str.php`.

> You can find the guidance documents and processes consisting of information related to STR in the developer guidelines at the following URL:
> `http://www.cups.org/documentation.php/spec-cmp.html`

Installing a Binary Distribution

You can also build binary packages that can be installed on other machines using the RPM spec file (`packaging/cups.spec`) or EPM list file (`packaging/cups.list`). The latter also supports building of binary RPMs (Red Hat Package Manager), which makes it more convenient to use.

Building RPMs

You can find the RPM software at `http://www.rpm.org/`.

The source distributions include an RPM spec file that can be used to build RPM packages for your Linux distribution. The `rpmbuild` command is used to build from the tar files:

```
#rpmbuild -ta cups-version-source.tar.gz
```

Or

```
#rpmbuild -ta cups-version-source.tar.bz2
```

You will need the `gcc`, `libjpeg`, `libjpeg-devel`, `libpng`, `libpng-devel`, `libtiff`, `libtiff-devel`, `zlib`, and `zlib-devel` packages installed to compile CUPS with all the standard functionalities. The `krb5-devel` and `krb5-libs` packages, `openldap` and `openldap-devel` packages, `openslp`, and `openslp-devel` packages will allow support for Kerberos (CUPS 1.3.x only), LDAP, and SLP respectively.

The spec file supports two options, `--without php` and `--without dbus`, which control whether the PHP and DBUS support is compiled into the packages. For example, if you are compiling CUPS 1.2.4 or earlier on Red Hat Enterprise Linux, you will need to provide the `--without dbus` option since that distribution does not have a compatible version of the D-BUS libraries available:

```
#rpmbuild -ta cups-version-source.tar.gz --without dbus
```

Similarly, if you don't have the `php-devel` package installed, then you can use the `--without the php` option to omit the PHP support from the generated RPMs.

```
#rpmbuild -ta cups-version-source.tar.gz --without php
```

Creating Binary Distribution with EPM

The EPM software is available at `http://www.easysw.com/epm/`.

The top level makefile supports generation of many types of binary distributions using EPM. To build a binary distribution type:

```
#make <format>
```

Or

```
#gmake <format>
```

For FreeBSD, NetBSD, and OpenBSD, the `<format>` target is one of the following:

- `epm` — Builds a script + tarfile package
- `aix` — Builds an AIX package
- `bsd` — Builds a BSD package
- `deb` — Builds a Debian package
- `depot` — Builds a HP-UX package (also swinstall)
- `inst` — Builds an IRIX package (also tardist)
- `osx` — Builds a MacOS X package
- `pkg` — Builds a Solaris package
- `rpm` — Builds a RPM package
- `setld` — Build a Tru64 UNIX package
- `slackware` — Build a Slackware package
- `swinstall` — Build a HP-UX package (also depot)
- `tardist` — Builds an IRIX package (also inst)

You can also use Google search engine to find other free binaries:

```
http://www.google.com/search?q=cups+binary+package&btnG=Search
```

> Mac OS X 10.5 comes with the CUPS 1.3. Cups1.3.x can be compiled and installed on the earlier versions of Mac OS X directly from source. Some GUI admin tools may not work properly in these versions.

Installing a Portable Distribution

To install the CUPS software from a portable distribution, you will need to login as root user. You can also use the su command to login as root user. Once the user is set as root the shell script should be run:

```
#./cups.install
```

After asking you a few yes/no questions, the CUPS software will be installed and the scheduler will be started automatically.

The su(switch user) can be used to change the ownership of a session to any user. It is most commonly employed to change the ownership from an ordinary user to the root user, thereby providing access to all parts, and all commands on the computer or system. For this reason, it is often referred to (although somewhat inaccurately) as the superuser command. It is also sometimes called the switch user command.

Installing an RPM Distribution

To install the CUPS software from an RPM distribution, you will need to be logged in as root user. As discussed earlier, doing a su login is also good enough. Once this is done, we can use the following commands to start installation:

```
#rpm -e lpr
#rpm -i cups-1.1-linux-M.m.n-intel.rpm
```

After a short delay, the CUPS software will be installed and the scheduler will be started automatically.

Installing CUPS from a Debian Distribution

To install the CUPS software from a Debian distribution, you will need to be logged in as the root user. Using the su is not good enough. Once you are logged in as the root user, you may run dpkg with:

```
#dpkg -i cups-1.1-linux-M.m.n-intel.deb
```

After a short delay, the CUPS software will be installed and the scheduler will be started automatically.

Subversion Access

The CUPS source files are managed by the Subversion (SVN) software, available at:

```
http://subversion.tigris.org/
```

Source files are "checked in" with each change so that modifications can be tracked. The CUPS software is available via Subversion using the following URL:

```
http://svn.easysw.com/public/cups/
```

The following command can be used to check the current CUPS 1.3.x source from Subversion:

```
#svn co http://svn.easysw.com/public/cups/branches/branch-1.3/cups-1.3.x
```

Similarly, the following command can be used to check the current CUPS 1.4.x source from Subversion:

```
#svn co http://svn.easysw.com/public/cups/trunk/cups
```

Compiling from Subversion

The CUPS Subversion repository does not hold a copy of the pre-built configure script. It requires running the GNU autoconf software (2.60 or higher) before compiling the software from Subversion:

```
#autoconf -f
```

Running the Software

Once the software is installed, the CUPS server can be started using the following command:

```
#/usr/sbin/cupsd
```

You can check whether CUPS is running using the following command:

```
#service cups status
```

Or

```
#ps -ax | grep cups
```

Installing CUPS Using the Package Manager on Linux

To install the CUPS software from the package manager available in the control center, click on **Install Software**. This will launch the package manager for software installation as shown in the following screenshot. Here, we have used the rpmdrake package manager of Mandriva (originally Mandrake) Distribution. The rpmdrake is a simple graphical frontend to manage software packages on a Mandriva Linux system. You can see the options for installation, removal and updation of software packages.

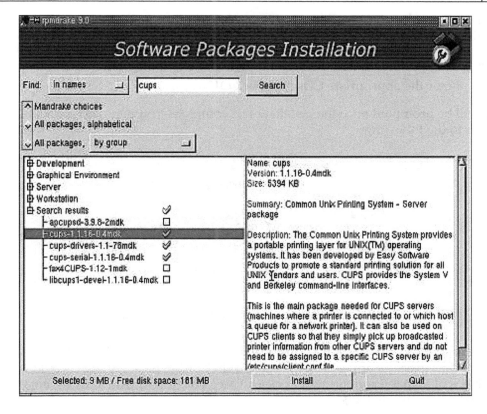

You can select the package that you want to install. The package can be selected by one of the following three options:

1. Search by choices
2. List by alphabetical order
3. All packages by group

Further, you should perform following steps to search for the desired package, **cups**:

*   Leave as default and enter the name of the application
*   Click on the **Search** button
*   On the search result, click on the correct package

 Some of the packages might require additional packages called dependencies. You can check out these dependencies by clicking on the main package and then reading the description to find out what dependencies that package may have (if any).

The installation options are displayed here. You can then perform the steps mentioned here:

- Click on **Install**
- Enter the appropriate CDs and Click **OK**

You will be prompted once the installation is complete. You may also see a warning similar to the following:

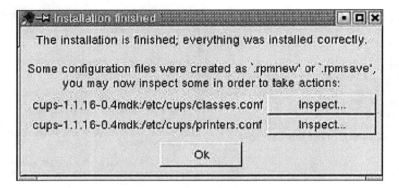

This message appears if you have just uninstalled CUPS, and trying to install it again. If this message appears on the screen, click on **Inspect** and remove the saved file that will help to keep the system clean. Once you have finished reviewing the installation notice, click **OK**.

Testing CUPS

We have seen various processes to install CUPS. Once installed, you should test CUPS to make sure whether it is working properly. Since CUPS uses the IPP (Internet Printing Protocol), you can verify this by opening a browser and typing `http://localhost:631/`.

The default port number on which CUPS listens is 631, but you can change it. We will see how to change this default port in Chapter 5 – *CUPS Server Management*.

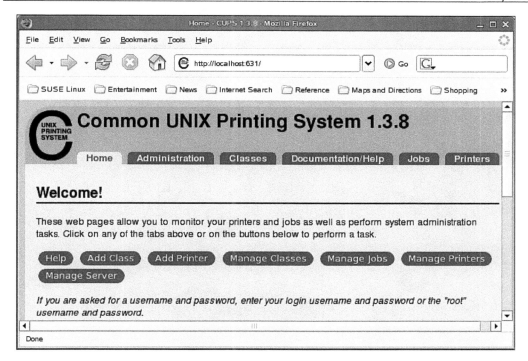

Summary

This chapter describes how to download the source code for CUPS, it also describes various methods for building and installing CUPS. The following are the various ways in which we can install CUPS, which we have discussed in the chapter:

- Using Source Code
- Binary Installation
- Using Subversion
- Using Package Manager

For the Binary Installation, we have also discussed the following scenarios for the installation.

- Using Portable Distribution
- RPM installation
- Debian Installation

Finally, we have seen how to access the CUPS server in a web browser using a special URL, so we can test it to see if it has been installed properly.

3

Printer Management

To manage printers in CUPS, the printer name and the driver for the printer are very important. In this chapter, we are going to discuss the various types of printer drivers that CUPS supports, and how to get and use them in CUPS. We will also discuss two highly popular methods for printer management — a command-line tool, and a web based graphical user interface (GUI).

Apart from these two, the KDEPrint and system-config printers are the utilities that are also used to add and manage printers. These utilities have their sets of screens that are more or less similar to the web interface of CUPS.

Printer Drivers

Printer drivers are pieces of software that convert the data to be printed in a form that can be understood by the printer. Printer drivers allow the applications to print without being aware of the technical details of each printer model that means "they are responsible for sending the characteristic information of the printer to the OS". Although, besides the PostScript language, CUPS understands other formats such as PDF, image, and text, but it normally converts them into PostScript.

PostScript Printer Description (PPD) Drivers

Let us first understand what is PostScript. PostScript is a platform-independent page description language which is used by many middle and high-end laser printers, and even by some high-end inkjet printers.

The PPD (Postscript Printer Description) files written in PostScript language are used by CUPS to describe printer technical details that are required by the OS to understand each printer model. Normally, PostScript printers are always shipped with appropriate PPD files, and these files describe their exact properties. Sometimes, these files are also used by the drivers for Windows and Mac OS. CUPS similar to the other open source applications (such as StarOffice, OpenOffice, GPR, and GIMP) use PPD to know about printer capabilities and other additional information.

In CUPS, PPD makes the full functionality of the printer (trays, resolutions, staplers, and so on) available, and that is why PPD is widely popular and highly recommended. All printers that CUPS can manage are described by the PPD files, whether they are able to output PostScript natively.

You can find the PPD files on the driver CDs that are shipped with printers. If you cannot unpack the driver from the manufacturer's CD, check the manufacturer's web site for a Linux driver version, or check the Open Printing or CUPS websites (URLs are given below):

- `http://openprinting.org/download/PPD/`
- `http://www.cups.org/ppd.php`

If you would like to learn more about PPD files, please visit the Linux Foundation website:

`http://www.linux-foundation.org/en/OpenPrinting/Database/PPDDocumentation`

Non-PostScript Printers

In UNIX and Linux, applications print using PostScript. Thus, all printers are assumed to be able to handle this functionality (printing with PostScript). If a printer does not understand PostScript then we require software that can be used to convert PostScript into a format that the printer can understand. Ghostscript is one such kind of interpreter which translates the incoming PostScript into the printer's own language.

Ghostscript Built-In

Ghostscript is an interpreter written in C language, which can run on various platforms including Mac and Windows. It is available on all UNIX and Linux platform to convert PostScript into the printer's desired form. CUPS filter normally calls Ghostscript. You can get more information about Ghostscript at:

`http://www.ghostScript.com/awki/Ghostscript`

The Ghostscript drivers are pieces of code compiled into the Ghostscript executable, so one has to rebuild Ghostscript to add a driver. Therefore, adding drivers for new printers is not trivial for most users, and it is not recommended to create new drivers of such type.

```
Last login: Fri Sep 19 14:17:03 2008 from 192.168.0.56
[root@cupsserver ~]# gs -h
GPL Ghostscript 8.60 (2007-08-01)
Copyright (C) 2007 Artifex Software, Inc.  All rights reserved.
Usage: gs [switches] [file1.ps file2.ps ...]
Most frequently used switches: (you can use # in place of =)
 -dNOPAUSE               no pause after page  | -q         `quiet`, fewer messages
 -g<width>x<height>      page size in pixels  | -r<res>    pixels/inch resolution
 -sDEVICE=<devname>      select device        | -dBATCH    exit after last file
 -sOutputFile=<file>     select output file: - for stdout, |command for pipe,
                                               embed %d or %ld for page #
Input formats: PostScript PostScriptLevel1 PostScriptLevel2 PostScriptLevel3 P
Default output device: display
Available devices:
   alc1900 alc2000 alc4000 alc4100 alc8500 alc8600 alc9100 ap3250 appledmp
   atx23 atx24 atx38 bbox bit bitcmyk bitrgb bitrgbtags bj10e bj10v bj10vh
   bj200 bjc600 bjc800 bjc880j bjccmyk bjccolor bjcgray bjcmono bmp16 bmp16m
   bmp256 bmp32b bmpgray bmpmono bmpsep1 bmpsep8 ccr cdeskjet cdj1600 cdj500
   cdj550 cdj670 cdj850 cdj880 cdj890 cdj970 cdjcolor cdjmono cfax cgm24
   cgm8 cgmmono chp2200 cif cljet5 cljet5c cljet5pr coslw2p coslwxl cp50
   cups declj250 deskjet devicen dfaxhigh dfaxlow display dj505j djet500
   djet500c dl2100 dnj650c epl2050 epl2050p epl2120 epl2500 epl2750 epl5800
   epl5900 epl6100 epl6200 eps9high eps9mid epson epsonc epswrite escp
   escpage faxg3 faxg32d faxg4 fmlbp fmpr fs600 gdi hl1240 hl1250 hl7x0
   hpdj1120c hpdj310 hpdj320 hpdj340 hpdj400 hpdj500 hpdj500c hpdj510
   hpdj520 hpdj540 hpdj550c hpdj560c hpdj600 hpdj660c hpdj670c hpdj680c
   hpdj690c hpdj850c hpdj855c hpdj870c hpdj890c hpdjplus hpdjportable ibmpro
   ijs imagen imdi inferno iwhi iwlo iwlq jetp3852 jj100 jpeg jpegcmyk
   jpeggray la50 la70 la75 la75plus laserjet lbp310 lbp320 lbp8 lex2050
   lex3200 lex5700 lex7000 lips2p lips3 lips4 lips4v lj250 lj3100sw lj4dith
   lj4dithp lj5gray lj5mono ljet2p ljet3 ljet3d ljet4 ljet4d ljet4pjl
   ljetplus ln03 lp1800 lp1900 lp2000 lp2200 lp2400 lp2500 lp2563 lp3000c
   lp7500 lp7700 lp7900 lp8000 lp8000c lp8100 lp8200c lp8300c lp8300f
   lp8400f lp8500c lp8600 lp8600f lp8700 lp8800c lp8900 lp9000b lp9000c
   lp9100 lp9200b lp9200c lp9300 lp9400 lp9600 lp9600s lp9800c
   lps4500 lps6500 lq850 lx5000 lxm3200 lxm5700m m8510 mag16 mag256 md1xMono
   md2k md50Eco md50Mono md5k mgr4 mgr8 mgrgray2 mgrgray4 mgrgray8 mgrmono
   miff24 mj500c mj6000c mj700v2c mj8000c ml600 necp6 npdl nullpage oce9050
   oki182 oki4w okiibm omni oprp opvp paintjet pam pbm pbmraw pcl3 pcx16
   pcx24b pcx256 pcx2up pcxcmyk pcxgray pcxmono pdfwrite pgm pgmraw pgnm
   pgnmraw photoex picty180 pj pjetxl pjxl pjxl300 pkm pkmraw pksm pksmraw
   plan9bm png16 png16m png256 png48 pngalpha pnggray pngmono pnm pnmraw ppm
   ppmraw pr1000 pr1000_4 pr150 pr201 ps2write psdcmyk psdrgb psgray psmono
   psrgb pswrite pxlcolor pxlmono r4081 rpdl samsunggdi sgirgb sj48 spotcmyk
   st800 stcolor sunhmono t4693d2 t4693d4 t4693d8 tek4696 tiff12nc tiff24nc
   tiff32nc tiffcrle tiffg3 tiffg32d tiffg4 tiffgray tifflzw tiffpack
   tiffsep uniprint wtscmyk wtsimdi x11 x11alpha x11cmyk x11cmyk2 x11cmyk4
   x11cmyk8 x11gray2 x11gray4 x11mono xcf xes
Search path:
   . : %rom%lib/ : /usr/share/ghostscript/8.60/lib :
   /usr/share/ghostscript/8.60/Resource : /usr/share/ghostscript/fonts :
   /usr/share/fonts/default/ghostscript : /usr/share/fonts/default/Type1 :
   /usr/share/fonts/default/amspsfnt/pfb :
   /usr/share/fonts/default/cmpsfont/pfb : /usr/share/fonts/japanese :
   /usr/share/ghostscript/conf.d : /etc/ghostscript : /etc/ghostscript/8.60
Initialization files are compiled into the executable.
For more information, see /usr/share/ghostscript/8.60/doc/Use.htm.
```

To determine which drivers are available, do `gs-h` and see the **devices** section of the output. The current Subversion repository of ESP Ghostscript contains all known free drivers of this type. You can learn how to download and install these drivers from:

```
http://www.linuxfromscratch.org/blfs/view/svn/pst/espgs.html
```

ESP Ghostscript is a versatile processor for PostScript data with the ability to render PostScript to different targets. ESP Ghostscript is a customized version of GNU Ghostscript that includes an enhanced configuration script, the CUPS raster driver to support CUPS raster printer drivers, and additional patches and drivers from various Linux distributors. You can find more information related to ESP Ghostscript at:

```
http://www.cups.org/espgs/index.php
```

Filter

A filter is a separate executable program that converts a printer-independent graphics format (PNM, PPM, and so on) produced by Ghostscript into the printer's native language. The main reason behind its existence is that quite a few people wanted to create a printer driver quickly without studying the internals of Ghostscript. The advantage with the filters is that they are not required to patch and compile Ghostscript for installation, and that makes the filter installation process very easy.

To find out whether the driver you need is already installed, you can use the following command which checks the driver's executable in the execution path:

```
$which <driver name>
```

CUPS Raster

CUPS raster is special kind of filter driver. To make the driver installation easy, CUPS uses Ghostscript to convert PostScript input into the CUPS raster format and additionally CUPS raster are used to convert the CUPS raster format into the printer's native language. The CUPS raster drivers always come with PPD files, and they contain not only the printer properties and options, but also instructions for CUPS to call correct CUPS filter.

In most of the Linux distribution, we can see which of these drivers are installed by looking at PPDs in the directory /usr/share/cups/model, but the location may vary depending upon the OS on which CUPS is installed, and also the printer model which appears while setting up print queue with the web-interface.

Ink Jet Server (IJS) Plug-in

The Ink Jet Server (IJS) plug-ins are newly developed, separate, executable programs, and they do not require Ghostscript to be patched and recompiled to add support to a new printer. Unlike CUPS raster, IJS plug-ins communicates bi-directionally with Ghostscript, and thus Ghostscript can ask them for certain printer properties and adapt their rendering appropriately. These executables have to be in the execution path, like filters. They usually contain ijs somewhere in their names. You can get more information about IJS plug-in at:

http://www.linuxprinting.org/ijs/

Uniprint

These are universal raster drivers that contain built-in drivers called uniprint in Ghostscript. You can supply all the commands which have to be sent to a printer for raster printing on the Ghostscript command line, or by a file:

For some printers there are several such files with the extension .upp in the /usr/share/GhostScript/<version>/lib/ directory.

CUPS DDK

The CUPS Driver Development Kit (DDK) is free software consisting of suites of standard drivers which provide interesting tools for building and manipulating PPD files. It also provides a PPD file compiler, other utilities which can be used for CUPS printer driver development and printing environment. It has a portable layer for printing for UNIX and Linux OS, and thus it also provides the means for mass -producing PPD files and drivers that can be used for CUPS.

The current version of the CUPS DDK is 1.2.3 and it can be downloaded from the CUPS web site:

http://www.cups.org/ddk/articles.php?L503

You can get its installation and configuration related information from the CUPS DDK manual:

http://www.cups.org/ddk/cupsddk.html

CUPS DDK is currently being merged into the core of CUPS and will be the part of CUPS 1.4 source code.

Foomatic-RIP

Foomatic-RIP is a universal print filter which is the internal component of the Foomatic runtime printing system. It works with many printing systems including CUPS. The following are some of the features of the Foomatic-RIP system:

- It has the capabilities for auto-detecting the system in which it analyzes the environment, and then it gets called, and can call printer drivers or filters with arbitrary command lines that have PostScript as standard input and the printer's language as standard output.

- Foomatic-RIP uses PPD files with extra keywords for non-PostScript printers. It also has advanced options which combine with PPD files. This combination is used for driver command line and the user-settable options. This way, it also adds PPD file support to non-CUPS printing systems.

- It has quite a few extra features such as page overrides (different option settings for selected pages), which make CUPS raster driver work with non-CUPS printing systems, and convert non-PostScript input data on non-CUPS printing systems.

You can get more information about how to install and download Foomatic-RIP from foomatic database at:

`http://www.linuxfoundation.org/en/OpenPrinting/Database/Foomatic`

 Foomatic-RIP (foomatic-filters) is a part of Foomatic database that also contains foomatic-db-engine, foomatic-db, and foomatic-db-hpijs.

Apart from this, CUPS also supports various other drivers such as Gutenprint, Turboprint, OpenPrinting Vector, and so on. Gutenprint, which was formally known as Gimp-print, can be downloaded from:

`http://gimp-print.sourceforge.net/`

CUPS also supports the printer-drivers for the Windows environment which can be downloaded from the CUPS website:

`http://www.cups.org/windows/index.php`

These drivers require us to use the `cupsaddsmb` command, which we will discuss in Chapter 6.

Installing PPD

As we know CUPS requires a PPD file to define how it will use the printer and the driver. So, if we have a PostScript printer, it just requires obtaining the PPD file from your printer's vendor. Typically, it will be somewhere in your vendor's driver box. As discussed earlier, we can also get PPD files from various other sources.

For non-PostScript printers, any of the above mentioned drivers should be downloaded, compiled, and installed. If you do not want to use any of the above mentioned non-PostScript drivers, then you can also use any other style of driver from your selected website. You can also get Foomatic PPDs which is nothing but a collection of many non-PostScript printers to function as if they were PostScript printers.

 Do not use Foomatic PPDs for PostScript printers when you have a manufacturer-supplied PPD. The Foomatic PPDs for PostScript printers are generic and support only a few options, whereas the manufacturer-supplied PPDs give access to the full functionality of your printer.

You can get Foomatic-PPD from the following URL. Once you select make and model and click on **Show** it will take you to a page were Foomatic-PPD for your printer can be downloaded:

http://www.linuxprinting.org/printer_list.cgi

To install a foomatic driver, look for the **Download PPD** links near the driver names on your printer's page. If a driver has no such link, then there is insufficient data to generate a PPD for the entry. In such a case, you need to see the text of the driver entry. Once the PPD is downloaded, it should be copied in the directory /usr/share/cups/model/ or a similar directory depending on our OS.

 The PPD file does not need to be executable, but it should be world-readable and should have the file name extension .ppd.

Then CUPS service needs to be reloaded to make these changes active, which can be done by executing one of following commands. Once the driver is installed, you can start adding the printer directly:

```
$sudo killall -HUP cupsd
```

Or

```
$sudo /etc/init.d/cups restart
```

Or

```
$sudo /sbin/service cups restart
```

> Sudo (superuser do) is a utility for Unix- and Linux-based systems that provides an efficient way to give specific users permission to use specific system commands at the root (most powerful) level of the system. Sudo also logs all commands and arguments.

Managing Printer through the Command Line

In order to add the printer, you must first check which printers are already available on the system, so as not to assign the new printer to a port that is already in use. To check the system for printers and their status, you can use the lpstat command. The following will allow you to see the status of all the printers on the system, as well as the scheduler and the jobs:

```
$lpstat -t
```

If your system does not have any printers installed currently, the output should look something like this:

scheduler is running
no system default destination

Once you have confirmed that the scheduler is running and the device you want to use is free, the next step is to add the printer using the lpadmin command. The lpadmin command allows you to perform most printer administration tasks from the command-line. It is normally located in /usr/sbin.

Basic Command for Adding the Printer

Setting up a printer correctly in CUPS depends on two critical choices—printer device name and printer driver. CUPS uses the lpadmin command to configure the printer and its classes. In this section, we will see various combinations of the lpadmin command, which performs operation such as adding a printer, modifying a printer, deleting a printer, and so on.

The following is the basic command to add a printer with its device-uri and ppd:

```
$sudo lpadmin -p printer -E -v device-uri -m ppd
```

Where:

Options	Description
-p	Configures the named printer.
-E	Enables the printer and accepts the job. This option is equivalent to running the `enable` and `accept` commands on the printer. These commands will be discuss later.
-v	It is used to set the device-uri attribute for the named printer. Here, device-uri is a uniform identifier for the printer.
-m model	Specifies a standard printer driver, which is usually a PPD file. PPDs are usually stored under the `/usr/share/cups/model/` directory structure.
	A list of all available models can be displayed using the `lpinfo` command with the `-m` option

In the following example, the printer "laserprinter" has been added with its driver that is a PPD file, `laser.ppd`, and its device-uri is "device". By default, this printer is configured to accept the job which is denoted by the `-E` option.

```
$sudo lpadmin -p laserprinter -E -v device -m laser.ppd
```

An inkjet printer connected to the parallel port, the command would look like this:

```
$sudo lpadmin -p inkjet -E -v parallel:/dev/lp1 -m inkjet.ppd
```

Similarly, a laser printer using a JetDirect network interface at IP address 192.168.0.3 would be added with the command:

```
$sudo lpadmin -p laserprinter -E -v socket:// 192.168.0.3 -m laser.ppd
```

For a dot matrix printer connected to the serial port, this might look like:

```
$sudo lpadmin -p DotMatrix -E -m dotMatrix.ppd \
  -v serial:/dev/ttyS0?baud=9600+size=8+parity=none+flow=soft
```

Here, you specify the serial port (such as S0, S1, d0, d1), baud rate (such as 9600, 19200, 38400, 115200, and so on), the number of bits, parity, and flow control. If you do not need flow control, delete the `+flow=soft` part.

In CUPS, while adding a printer you can also supply the information for printer's location and description. These will help you recognizing appropriate printer in organization. To add information about the Location and a Description of the printer:

```
$sudo lpadmin -p cupsprinter -L "Production Dept. 3rd Floor"
  -D "ColourNetwork\ Printer"
```

Options	Description
-L location	It provides a textual location for the printer
-D info	It provides a textual description of the printer

Managing Printers from the Command-Line

The following are the some of very useful options that can be used with the `lpadmin` command for adding and modifying printers. You must run the `lpadmin` command with the `-p` option to add or modify a printer:

```
$sudo lpadmin -p printer options
```

Where:

Options	Description
-c class	It is used to add the named printer to a printer class. If the class does not exist, then it is created. We will discuss this in the next chapter.
-i interface	It copies the named *interface* script to the printer. Interface scripts are used by System V printer drivers. Since all filtering is disabled when using an interface script, scripts generally should not be used unless there is no other driver for a printer.
	This option cannot be specified with the *-P* option (PPD file), and is intended for providing support for legacy printer drivers.
-r class	It removes the named printer from the printer class. If the resulting class becomes empty, then it is removed.
-P ppd-file	It specifies a local PPD file for the printer driver.

[We can get more information about `lpadmin` options from the man page: `http://www.cups.org/documentation.php/man-lpadmin.html`]

Deleting Printers

You should run the `lpadmin` command with the `-x` option to delete a printer:

```
$sudo lpadmin -x printer
```

The following example will delete the printer `cupsprinter`:

```
$sudo lpadmin -x cupsprinter
```

Setting the Default Printer

You should run the `lpadmin` command with the `-d` option to set a default printer:

```
$sudo lpadmin -d printer
```

```
$sudo lpadmin -d cupsprinter
```

The above example will set the `cupsprinter` printer as the default one:

 The default printer can be overridden by the user using the `lpoptions` command.

Starting and Stopping Printers

The `cupsenable` and `cupsdisable` commands start and stop printer queues, respectively:

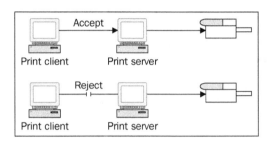

```
$sudo cupsenable printer cupsprinter
```

The above command will make the requested printer, `cupsprinter`, active. This printer is now ready to accept jobs.

```
$sudo cupsdisable -d "Changing the properties" cupsprinter
```

The above command will make `cupsprinter` disabled because of the given reason, and it will not print any job.

 Printers that are disabled may still accept jobs for printing, but won't actually print any file until they are restarted. This is useful if the printer malfunctions, and you need time to correct the problem. Any queued jobs are printed after the printer is enabled (started).

Accepting and Rejecting Print Jobs

The `accept` and `reject` commands accept and reject print jobs for the named printer respectively:

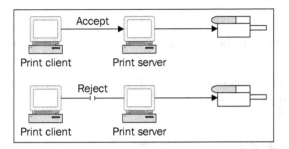

```
$sudo accept cupsprinter
```

This command will make `cupsprinter` printer ready to accept print jobs:

```
$sudo reject -r "It is down for repair" cupsprinter
```

Here, the destination printer, that is, the `cupsprinter`, is no longer accepting jobs. Here, `-r` is used to specify the reason.

As noted above, a printer can be stopped, but will still accept new print jobs. A printer can also reject new print jobs while it finishes those that have been queued. This is useful when you must perform maintenance on the printer, and will not have it available to users for a long period of time.

Checking Printer Status

Many routine printer administration tasks require you to know the status of the print service or a specific printer. For example, you can determine which printers are available for use and can examine the characteristics of those printers. You can use the `lpstat` command to find the status information about the print service or a specific printer.

The following example shows how to display the system's default printer:

```
$lpstat -d
```

system default destination: cupsprinter

The following example shows how to display the status of the printer:

```
$lpstat -p cupsprinter -r
```

printer cupsprinter is idle. enabled since Mar 27 11:17 2008. available.

Setting Quotas on a Printer

CUPS supports page and size-based quotas for each printer. The quotas are tracked individually for each user, but a single set of limits applies to all users for a particular printer. For example, if you limit printing on a particular printer to 5 pages per day, it will apply to all the users. You cannot set different limits for different users on a given printer. We will also discuss this in detail in Chapter 7 — *Setting up Quotas with CUPS*.

Restricting User Access to a Printer

The -u option of the lpadmin command controls which users can print to a printer. The default configuration allows all users to print to a printer:

```
$sudo lpadmin -p cupsprinter -u allow:all
```

CUPS supports allow and deny lists so that you can specify a list of users who are allowed to print, or not allowed to print. Along with your list of users, you can specify whether they are allowed or not allowed to use the printer. We will discuss the user level restrictions in Chapter 7.

Printing Banner Pages

A banner page identifies who submitted the print request, the print job ID, and when the job was printed. A banner page will also have a modifiable title to help users identify their printouts.

Banner pages make identifying the owner of a print job easy, which is especially helpful when many users submit jobs to the same printer. Printing banner pages uses more paper, however, and might not be necessary if a printer has only a few users. In some cases, printing banner pages is undesirable. For example, if a printer has special paper or forms mounted such as paycheck forms, printing banner pages might cause problems.

By default, the print service forces banner pages to be printed. However, you can give users a choice to turn off printing a banner page when they submit a print request. You can set this choice through the lpadmin command. If you give the users a choice, they have to use the -o banner option to turn off banner page printing.

Also, if you don't need or want banner pages, you can turn off banner pages so they are never printed. You can turn off banner page printing by using the lpadmin command.

You can make Banner Pages optional using the following command:

```
$sudo lpadmin -p cupsprinter -o banner=optional
```

Printing Banner Pages option can also be turned off using the following command:

```
$sudo lpadmin -p cupsprinter -o banner=never
```

Some More Printer and CUPS-Specific Commands

You can find out CUPS related man pages that are present on your system:

```
$apropos cups
```

There are also some printer specific options that will be processed by the printer itself. You can get a list of options that the printer supports via its Postscript Printer Description (PPD) with `lpoptions`.

```
$lpoptions -p cupsprinter -l
```

The output gives the properties of the `cupsprinter` (where `cupsprinter` is the name of the printer). It can be changed with the command line switch `-o`.

The command `lpoptions` can also make an instance of a printer for the user, so you can have an easy way to store multiple configurations for a single printer. When you create an instance for a printer or use `lpoptions`, it will modify a file in your home directory called `lpoptions`. This is where it stores all the options that you create.

To create an instance of a printer you just need to give the `lpoptions` command with the printer, but append a backslash character "/" and a name, and give it the options you want to associate with the instance. For example:

```
$lpoptions -p cupsprinter/noduplex -o Duplex=none
```

The above command will create an instance name "noduplex" that does not have duplex printing disabled. You can then use this instance name whenever you want to print without duplexing option.

This will create an instance that you can then use as the printer name and get the options that you want without having to remember them every time you want a print. You can now use the instance in your print commands such as `lp` or `lpr` in place of the printer name.

You can get more information about lpoption in the man page: http://www.cups.org/documentation.php/man-lpoptions. html?TOPIC=Man+Pages

Managing Print Jobs through Command Line

One of the most useful features in CUPS is its ability to manage print jobs. This section deals with the various features CUPS offers to manage print jobs via the command line interface.

Submitting Files for Printing

CUPS provides both the System V lp and Berkeley lpr for printing commands. You need to type the following command to print a file to the default printer on your system.

```
$lp file
```

or

```
$lpr file
```

As we know, CUPS can understand various types of files directly that include PostScript, text, PDF, and image files. This allows you to print from within your applications or through the command-line.

Checking the Status of Print Jobs

The following example shows that user kajol has one print request queued to the printer CUPSLaser:

```
$lpstat
```

cupsprinter-1   kajol   1261   Mar 17 19:48

The following example shows that the user kajol currently has no print requests in queue:

```
$lpstat -u kajol
```

The following example shows that two print requests are queued on the printer `cupsprinter`:

```
$lpstat -o cupsprinter
```

kajol-87   root   1024   Mar 27 09:07

kajol-88   root   1024   Mar 27 09:08

Choosing a Printer

Many systems will have more than one printer available to the user. These printers can be attached to the local system via a parallel, serial, or USB port, or it can be available over the network.

We can use the `lpstat` command to see a list of available printers:

```
$lpstat -p -d
```

The `-p` option specifies that you want to see a list of printers, and the `-d` option reports the current default printer or class.

We can use the `-d` option with the `lp` command to print to a specific printer:

```
$lp -d cupsprinter file
```

or the `-P` option with the `lpr` command:

```
$lpr -P cupsprinter file
```

Setting Printer Options

For many types of files, the default printer options may be sufficient for your needs. However, there may be times when you need to change the options for a particular file you are printing.

The `lp` and `lpr` commands allow you to pass printer options using the `-o` option:

```
$lp -o landscape -o scaling=75 -o media=A4 filename.jpg
$lpr -o landscape -o scaling=75 -o media=A4 filename.jpg
```

Option	Description
-o landscape	It is a generic option.
–o scaling = number	It is used to scale image files to use upto some percent of the page. If the value of percent is greater than 100, then the image file will be printed across multiple pages.
–o media = size	It is used to set the page size to the size with a mention argument. Most of printers support the sizes "A4", "letter", and "legal".

 The available printer options may vary depending on the printer. You can check standard printing options at the CUPS website: `http://www.cups.org/documentation.php/options.html#OPTIONS`

Printing the Output of a Program

The following two `lp` commands print from the standard input to the default printer and the `cupsprinter` respectively:

```
$program | lp
$program | lp -d cupsprinter
```

The following `lpr` commands support printing from the standard input:

```
$program | lpr
$program | lpr -P cupsprinter
```

In both the cases, if the program does not provide any output, then nothing will be queued for printing.

Printing Multiple Copies

The `lp` and `lpr` commands can also be used with the following options for printing more than one copy of a file:

```
$lp -n num-copies file
$lpr -#num-copies file
```

Here `-n` is used to specify the number of copies for the file. It should be in the range of 1 to 100. The copies are normally not collated for you. Use the `-o Collate=True` option to get collated copies:

```
$lp -n num-copies -o Collate=True file
$lpr -#num-copies -o Collate=True file
```

There are other generic options available in the man pages of these commands. They are available at:

`http://www.cups.org/documentation.php/man-lp.html?TOPIC=Man+Pages`

`http://www.cups.org/documentation.php/man-lpr.html?TOPIC=Man+Pages`

Checking the Printer Status

The `lpstat` command without any option can be used to check for active jobs that you have submitted for printing:

```
$lpstat
```

The jobs are listed in the order they will be printed. Use the `-p` option to see which files and printers are active:

```
$lpstat -p
```

Use the `-o` and `-p` options together to show the jobs and the printers:

```
$lpstat -o -p
```

Canceling a Print Job

You can use the `cancel` command to cancel print requests from printer queues or to cancel jobs that are printing. Three ways to use the cancel command are as follows:

- Cancel the requests using job identification number (job ID)
- Cancel the job from a specific user on all or specific printers
- Cancel the job currently printing

When you use the `cancel` command, a message tells you that the jobs are cancelled, and the next job in queue is printed. You can cancel a print request only if you are:

- The user who submitted the job, and you are logged in on the system from which you submitted the job
- The user who submitted the job on any client system and the print server has the `user-equivalence` option configured for the printer in its `/etc/printers.conf` file
- Logged in as superuser or `su`, or have assumed an equivalent role on the print server

To cancel a specific request, you need to know its job ID. The job ID contains the name of the printer, a dash, and the number of the print request, for example, `cupspinter-87`.

When you submit the print job, the job ID is displayed. If you do not remember the print job ID, you can find it by using the `lpstat` command with the `-o` printer option.

We can use `cancel` or `lprm` commands to cancel a print job:

```
$cancel job-id
$lprm job-id
```

Here, the `job-id` is the number that was reported to you by the `lp` or `lpstat` commands. You can find out more information about these commands in the manual pages:

http://www.cups.org/documentation.php/man-cancel.html?TOPIC=Man+Pages

http://www.cups.org/documentation.php/man-lprm.html?TOPIC=Man+Pages

You can verify whether the print job is cancelled using the following command:

```
$lpstat -o cupsprinter
```

You can use the `lp` and `lpr` commands to set the printer's options such as selecting the banner page, setting the orientation, selecting the range of pages and so on. CUPS has divided these options into different categories such as General, Banner, Document, and Text. Setting up these options are easier to manage through the web interface rather than trying to use the command line. We will see how to do this later in the chapter while discussing the "Managing Printers using the CUPS Web Interface" section.

Moving a Print Job

If you plan to change the way a printer is used or decide to take a printer out of service, you should set up the CUPS service to reject additional print requests. Then, move or cancel any request that is currently queued to the printer. You can use the lpmove command to move individual or all print requests to another local printer.

Job IDs are not changed when you move print requests, so users can still find their requests. Print requests that have requirements, such as file content type that cannot be met by the newly specified printer cannot be moved. These print requests must be canceled:

```
$sudo lpmove cupsprinter1 cupsprinter2
```

Before executing the above command, we need to check Job IDs of Print requests on the original printer, that is cupsprinter1.

```
$lpstat -o cupsprinter1
```

Also, we need to verify whether cupsprinter2 is accepting print jobs:

```
$lpstat -p cupsprinter2
```

The following command moves all the jobs from cupsprinter1 to cupsprinter2:

The lpmove command is located in the system command directory typically /usr/sbin or /usr/local/sbin, and so may not be in your command path. Specify the full path to the command if you get a **command not found** error. For example: /usr/sbin.

Managing Printers using the CUPS Web Interface

In this section, we will discuss above mentioned functions related to printer and job using CUPS web interface.

The CUPS web server provides a user-friendly interface for adding your printers. Rather than figure out which device URI and PPD files to use, you can instead click on the appropriate listings and fill in some simple information. Enter the following URL in your web browser to begin: http://localhost:631/admin.

The following screen should appear within your browser. We can see a number of tabs such as **Administration, Classes, Documentation/Help, Jobs,** and **Printers** within this page.

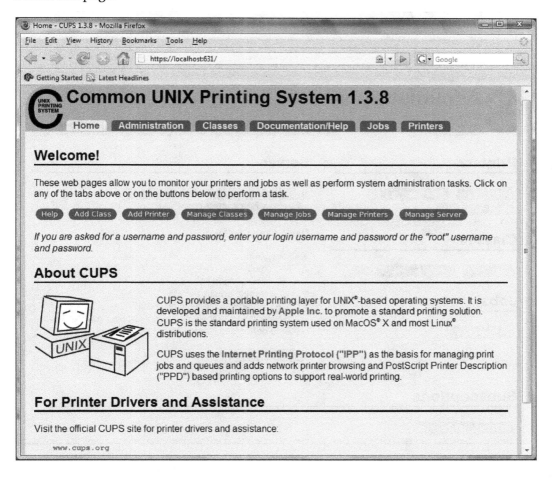

Administration

The administration window in the CUPS web interface looks like this:

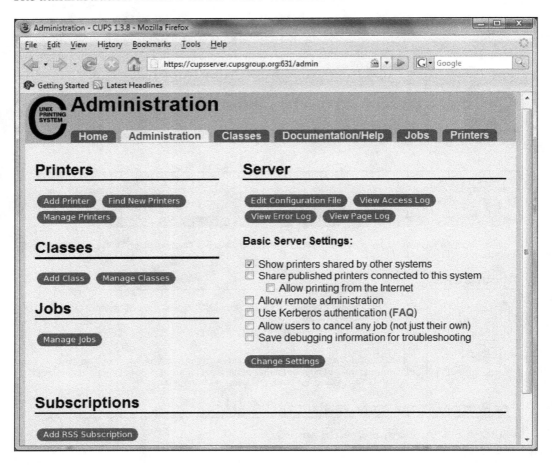

Adding a New Printer

Clicking on **Add Printer** shows you the following screen:

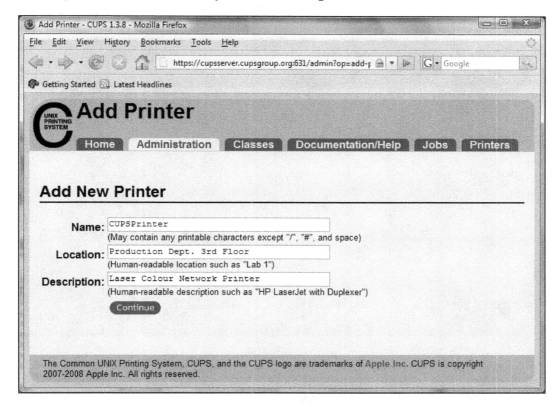

You will need to fill in an appropriate name for your printer. You can also specify the location, and a description for the given printer which helps people recognize the printer. But these fields are not mandatory and can be kept blank.

The printer name must start with any printable character except " ", "/", and "@". It can contain up to 127 letters, numbers, and the underscore (_). Case is not significant, for example, "CUPSPRINTER", "CUPSPrinter", and "cupsprinter" are all considered to be the same. Once this is done, click on the **Continue** option.

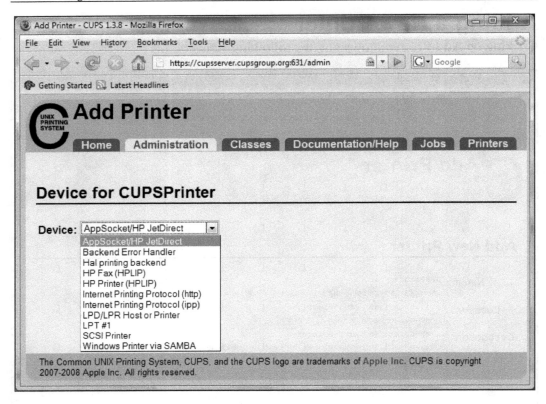

AppSocket/HP JetDirect uses this to print from a printer that is connected to JetDirect box. This backend sends print files to AppSocket (a.k.a., HP JetDirect) connected network printers. An example for the CUPS device-URI to use is `socket://10.11.12.13:9100`.

> A URI (Uniform Resource Identifier) is an identifier consisting of a sequence of characters. Depending on how you communicate with your device, the device URI needs to be specified.

Backend Error Handler (BEH) is used to handle the errors that occur between CUPS backends and the Printer. The BEH works with every backend except with the hp backend from HPLIP.

```
beh:/1/3/5/socket://printer:9100

beh:/0/10/60/socket://printer:9100
```

Scenario: One of the problems for home/desktop users is that they often switch their printers on only when they really want to print (to save energy). There is a common scenario that they send a job and forget to switch on the printer. CUPS disables the queue and the annoying re-enabling procedure has to be done. And many users do not know even about the problem. So the printer does not print and the queue gets nuked and re-created. People look for solutions on the help forums, or at the installation support of their distributions.

This problem can be easily avoided by installing BEH, the Backend Error Handler. This script makes the handling of such backend errors configurable, so that the problem can easily be worked around.

HP Printer (HPLIP) is a complete imaging and printing system for CUPS that includes HPIJS. It has built-in support for the scanner and card-reader, among other things. It also allows you to monitor ink levels, which is quite useful. If your only concern is printing, it is recommended to use hpijs that has no dependencies other than cups and foomatic. This hpijs is the basic printing driver that supports printing from CUPS, LPD, PPR, and other spoolers

HPLIP a successor to hpoj is a collection of optimized drivers for HP printers, and it is not just another component, as some people seem to think. If you are still using HPOJ, an up grade is highly recommended.

HPIJS is a subcomponent of HPLIP. HPIJS provides basic printing support for non-postscript printers. HPIJS can operate in any spooler environment (including no spooler).

HPIJS provides no I/O whereas HPLIP provides I/O for bi-directional communication, scanning, photo card access, and toolbox functionality. HPLIP requires the CUPS spooler.

```
hp:/net/$SED_OUTPUT?ip=nnn.nnn.nnn.nnn
```

It looks like this:

hp:/net/Photosmart_2600_series?ip=192.168.1.5

HP Fax (HPLIP) is used to configure printer for HP Fax:

```
hpfax:/usb/psc_2500_series?serial=XXXXXXXXX (HP psc_2500_series)
```

Internet Printing Protocol (IPP) is use to print to a remote CUPS server, or to print to a Windows computer with IIS and the IPP ISAPI DLL installed. This backend sends print files to IPP-connected network printers (or to other CUPS servers). Examples of CUPS device-URIs to use are `ipp::://192.193.194.195/ipp` (for many HP printers) and `ipp://remote_cups_server/printers/remote_printer_name`.

Internet Printing Protocol (HTTP) is used to print to a CUPS server same as IPP. This backend sends print files to HTTP-connected printers. (The `http://` CUPS backend is only a symlink to the `ipp://` backend.) Examples for the CUPS device-URIs to use are `http::://192.193.194.195:631/ipp` (for many HP printers) and `http://remote_cups_server:631/printers/remote_printer_name`.

LPD/LPR Host or Printer uses this to print to a remote LPD/LPR host which includes Windows 2000 installations that have the Print Services for UNIX CUPS Installation. An example for the CUPS device-URI to use is `lpd://remote_host_name/remote_queue_name`.

LPT #1 uses this to print to the local LPT port. If this option is not available, then your LPT port might be disabled in the BIOS. This backend sends print files to printers connected to the parallel port. An example of the CUPS device-URI to use is `parallel:/dev/lp0`.

Serial backend sends the specified job to a local printer connected via the specified serial port device. The URI is of the form: `serial:/dev/file?option [+option+...]`. The options are baud, bits, flow, and so on.

USB backend sends the specified job to a local printer connected via the specified usb port device. The URI is of the form: `usb:/dev/file`

SCSi Printer uses this to print the SCSI interface. An example for the CUPS device-URI to use is `scsi:/dev/sr1`.

Windows Printer via SAMBA uses to print files to printers shared by a Windows host. Examples of CUPS device-URIs that may be used includes:

`smb://workgroup/server/printersharename`

`smb://server/printersharename`

`smb://username:password@workgroup/server/printersharename`

`smb://username:password@server/printersharename`

It is easy to write your own backend as shell or Perl scripts if you need any modification or extension to the CUPS print system. One reason could be that you want to create special printers that send the print jobs as email (through a `mailto:/` backend), convert them to PDF (through a `pdfgen:/` backend) or dump them to `/dev/null`.

Caution Regarding USB Printers

CUPS requires the users to insure that the desired USB printer is powered on and physically connected to the USB bus before starting the CUPS software.

CUPS must see the USB printer when the software starts. The CUPS software is typically started when the computer boots. If the USB printer was not connected and powered on at the time CUPS was started, there will not be a USB printer shown in the list of devices on the CUPS Admin Device Window. If this happens, stop the CUPS software, properly connect and power on the USB printer, and restart the CUPS software

Once you select proper backend, click on **Continue**. You can see the following screen.

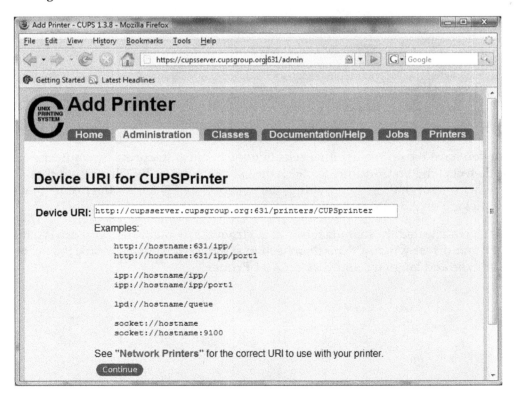

You then need to provide proper/desired **Device URI**. If you click on **Continue**, you will see the following window:

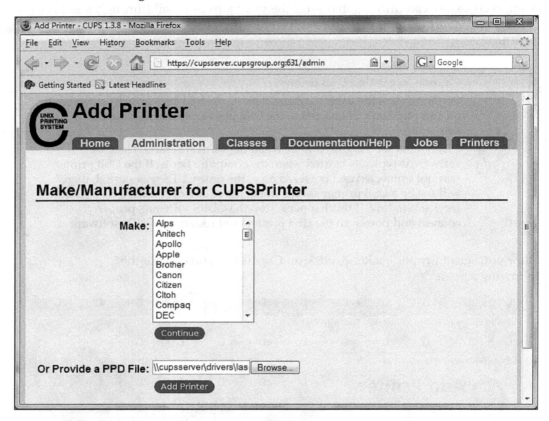

Here you have the option of either selecting the name of the printer manufacturer and then clicking on **Continue** to check the list of available PPD drivers for that manufacturer, or of directly providing the path of the PPD file for the printer and then clicking on **Add Printer**, which will ask for authentication.

If you have selected the manufacturer name from the available list, you can see the model and driver window. You then need to select the proper driver for the proper model type and language and click on **Add Printer**.

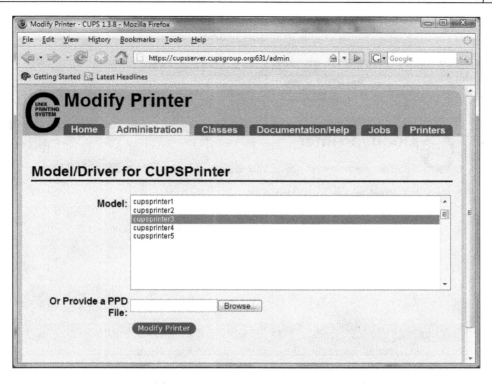

You need to provide the correct username and password to allow the printer to be added in the CUPS management panel. Here you can use the root user or the username having sufficient permissions to manage CUPS administration.

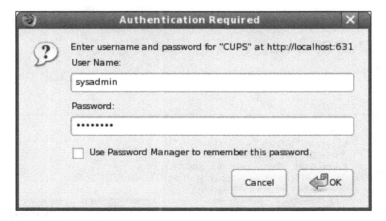

Once you have entered the correct username and password, the following screen will appear:

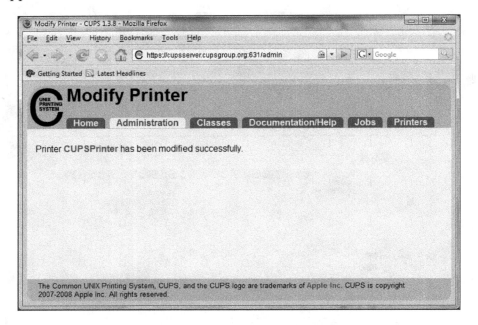

The default state of the printer is **idle, accepting jobs, published**.

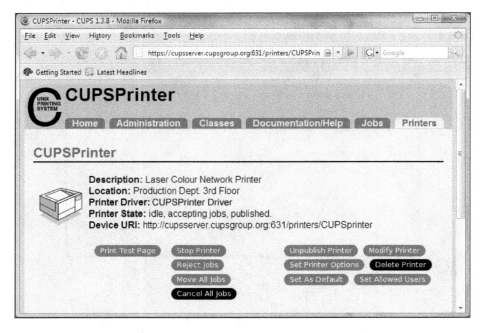

We can see a number of options with the printer:

Print Test Page prints the test page on your printer. **Set As Default** makes the printer a default one.

Stop Printer stops the printer which coverts printer state into stopped and also activates the option **Start Printer** that puts the printer again into an idle state.

Reject jobs converts the printer state into rejecting job and activates the option **Accept Jobs** that will put printer into a state where it is ready to accept jobs.

The option **Unpublished Printer** turns the printer unpublished, which means that the printer is no longer shared. **Published printer** option puts the printer into a shared mode. The default value is **true** which means the printer is in shared mode.

Delete All Jobs deletes all the jobs that are currently in queue, while **Delete Printer** deletes the printer with its entire configuration from the CUPS Administration Panel. Both these options ask for user authentication.

Modify Printer allows you to takes all the screen used in the **Adding Printer** option in which you can modify fields such as **Location**, **Description** of that printer.

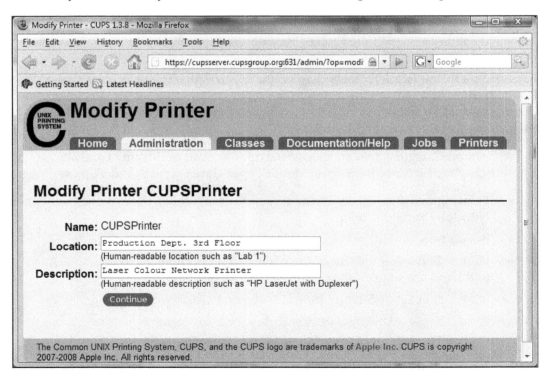

Move All Jobs allows you to shift all the jobs from one printer to another.

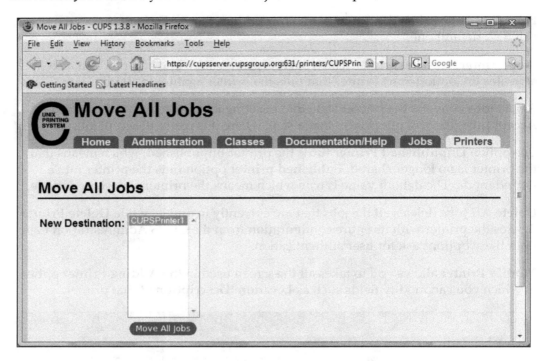

Set Printer Option is solely dependent on the features that the printers support. In this section, you will get the different options based on the driver you chose. In our example for the CUPSprinter, it shows four main categories: **General**, **Miscellaneous**, **Banners**, and **Policies**.

In the **General** Category, we can specify the options such as Printing Quality, Resolution, Page Size, Media Source, Media Type, Transparency, and Copies.

- **Printing quality** denotes the quality of printing. It has options such as Normal, Draft, and so on.

- **Resolution** is nothing but dots per inch (dpi).

- **Page Size** defines the size of the paper that the printer supports. The following are some of the options for the Page size.

    ◦ Letter—US Letter (8.5x11 inches, or 216x279mm)

    ◦ Legal—US Legal (8.5x14 inches, or 216x356mm)

    ◦ A4—ISO A4 (8.27x11.69 inches, or 210x297mm)

    ◦ COM10—US #10 Envelope (9.5x4.125 inches, or 241x105mm)

    ◦ DL—ISO DL Envelope (8.66x4.33 inches, or 220x110mm)

- **Media Source** is the location where media (e.g. paper) can be drawn from. This will vary from printer to printer. The following are some of the options for the media source.

  ° `Upper`—Upper paper tray

  ° `Lower`—Lower paper tray

  ° `Multipurpose`—Multi-purpose paper tray

  ° `LargeCapacity`—Large capacity paper tray

  ° `Manual feed`

  ° `Media Type` specifies the type of media for example `Transparency`, `Standard`, `PaperPostcard`, and `Thick Stock`.

- **Copies** refer to the default value for the number of copies to print for each job request. It can vary from 1 to 100.

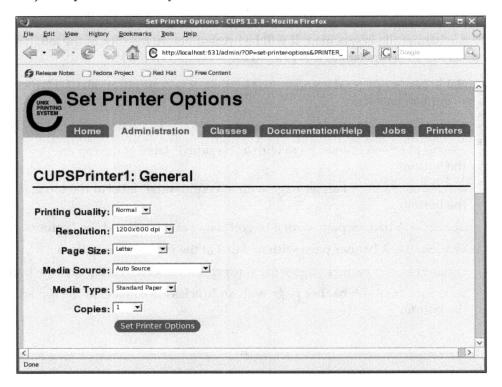

In the **Miscellaneous** category, options such as N-up printing and N-up Orientation are used.

`N-up Printing` is the feature that allows you to compose multiple page documents into one single page. CUPS supports 1, 2, 4, 6, 9, and 16-Up formats. The default format is 1-Up.

`N-up Orientation` includes the following orientation options such as Landscape, Portrait, Seascape, and so on:

- `Landscape` — 90 degree rotation
- `Portrait` — It means no rotation
- `Seascape` or `reverse landscape` — 270 degrees rotation
- `Reverse portrait` or `upside-down` — 180 degrees rotation

Banners include the `Starting Banner` and `Ending Banner` for the printer.

If only one banner file is specified, it will be printed before the files in the job. If a second banner file is specified, it is printed after the files in the job.

The available banner pages depend on the local system configuration; CUPS includes the following banner files:

- `none` — It does not produce a banner page
- `classified` — A banner page with a "classified" label at the top and the bottom
- `confidential` — A banner page with a "confidential" label at the top and the bottom
- `Secret` — A banner page with a "secret" label at the top and the bottom
- `standard` — A banner page with no label at the top and the bottom
- `topsecret` — A banner page with a "topsecret" label at the top and the bottom
- `unclassified` — A banner page with an "unclassified" label at the top and the bottom

Policy is nothing but the sets of rules that apply for the printer. It includes the options, `Error Policy` and `Operation Policy`.

`Error Policy` field is used to specify the error policy when there is an error in the printer while printing a job. In this policy, you can use options such as "stop-printer", "retry-job", and "abort-jobs".

`Operation Policy` is the field that denotes the printing policy of the printer. You can specify here whether the printer is set to be default or not.

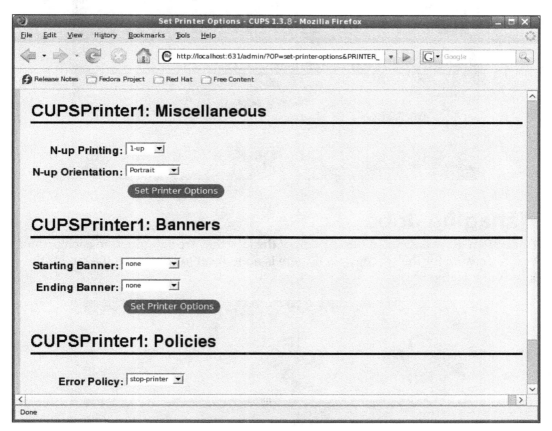

Set Allowed Users is used to allow or prevent users from having access to the printer. Here you can specify multiple users (separated by a comma) who should be authorized for having this printer access. We will discuss this in Chapter 7.

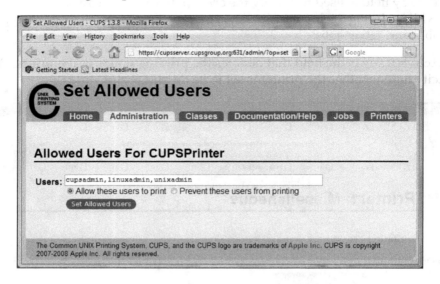

Managing Jobs

This option gives a detailed description of the jobs that are submitted to each printer. You can search for the specific job. If there is no request for the print, the tab for the **Jobs** will look like this:

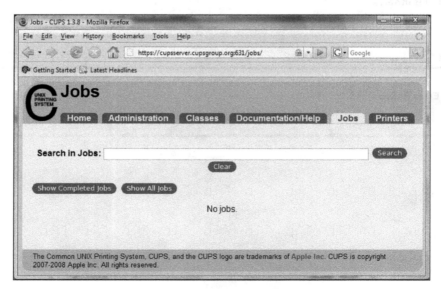

But if the user has sent the request to print, you can see that print request in the **Jobs** tab as an active job, as shown in the following screenshot. You can cancel, move, or reprint a particular job while it is "active".

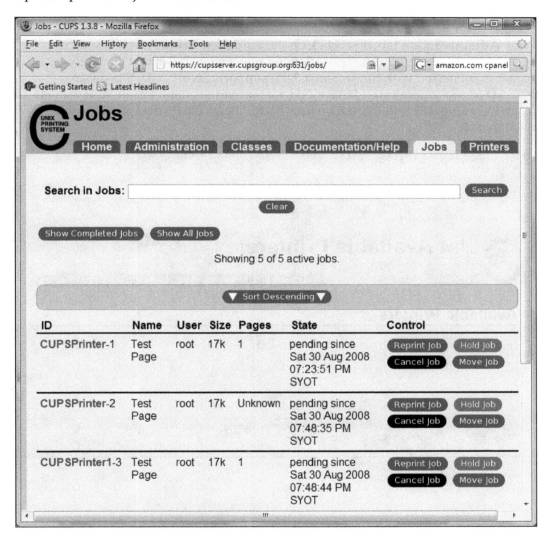

You can also see the already completed jobs and the status of all the jobs using the options, **Show Completed Jobs** and **Show All Jobs** respectively.

Find New Printers

In the **Administration** tab, if we click on the **Find New Printers**, it will search for newly connected printers. The following screenshot shows that currently no printer is connected with the system. CUPS supports SNMP, CUPS browsing, DNS-SD (*Bonjour/Zeroconf*), LDAP *w/SSL* to discover printers. The default value is CUPS browsing. We will discuss on how SNMP helps CUPS discovering printers in Chapter 8.

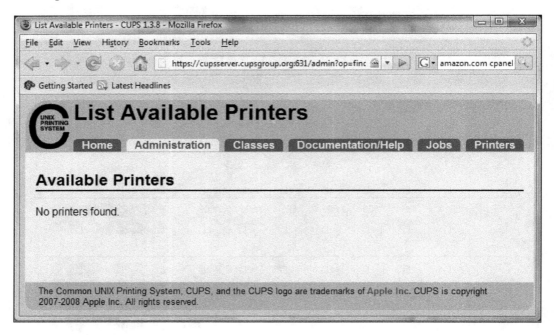

If any printer is connected to the CUPS server, the search wizard will show the list of available printers as follows. You can then use **Add This Printer** option to add a printer.

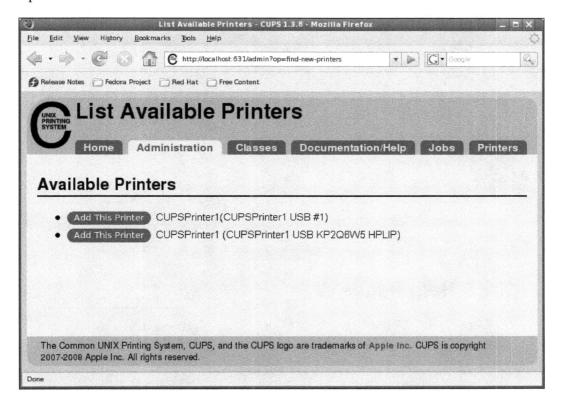

Documentation

At any point, if you need any help for the documentation, or man pages, you can use the **Documentation/Help** tab, or you can visit the documentation section of the CUPS website for the latest update:

```
http://www.cups.org/documentation.php
```

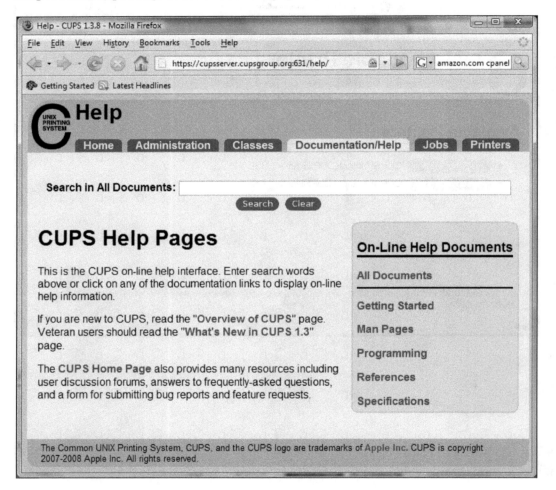

Summary

In this chapter, we have seen various ways to add and manage printers using CUPS. The command line interface—lpadmin and web interface are two widely used methods that we have looked at in detail. In the next chapter, we will see how to work with and manage printer classes.

4

Managing Multiple Printers at a Time

Unlike other printing systems, CUPS features a way to let you select a group of printers to print a job instead of selecting just one. In that way, if one printer is busy or down, another printer can be automatically selected to perform the job. Such groupings of printers are called **printer classes**.

Configuring Printer Classes

By default there are no printer classes set up. You will need to define them. The following are some of the criteria you can use to define printer classes:

- **Printer Type**: Printer type can be a PostScript or non-PostScript printer.
- **Location**: The location can describe the printer's place; for example the printer is placed on the third floor of the building.
- **Department**: Printer classes can also be defined on the basis of the department to which the printer belongs. The printer class might contain several printers that are used in a particular order.

CUPS always checks for an available printer in the order in which printers were added to a class. Therefore, if you want a high-speed printer to be accessed first, you would add the high-speed printer to the class before you add a low-speed printer. This way, the high-speed printer can handle as many print requests as possible, and the low-speed printer would be reserved as a backup printer when the high-speed printer is in use.

It is not compulsory to add printers in classes. There are a few important tasks that you need to do to manage and configure printer classes.

Printer classes can themselves be members of other classes. So it is possible for you to define printer classes for high availability for printing. Once you configure the printer class, you can print to the printer class in the same way that you print to a single printer.

Features and Advantages

Here are some of the features and advantages of printer classes in CUPS:

- Even if a printer is a member of a class, it can still be accessed directly by users if you allow it. However, you can make individual printers reject jobs while groups accept them. As the system administrator, you have control over how printers in classes can be used.

- The replacement of printers within the class can easily be done. Let's understand this with the help of an example.

  You have a network consisting of seven computers running Linux, all having CUPS installed. You want to change printers assigned to the class. You can remove a printer and add a new one to the class in less than a minute. The entire configuration required is done as all other computers get their default printing routes updated in another 30 seconds. It takes less than one minute for the whole change—less time than a laser printer takes to warm up.

- Let's take one more example to get to know about the advantages of "printer classes":

  A company is having the following type of printers with their policy as:

    ° A class for B/W laser printers that anybody can print on

    ° A class for draft color printers that anybody can print on, but with restrictions on volume

    ° A class for precision color printers that is unblocked only under the administrator's supervision

  All of these printers hang off Windows machines, and would be available directly for other computers running under Windows. However, we get the following advantages by providing them through CUPS on a central router:

    ° CUPS provide the means for centralizing printers, and users will only have to look for a printer in a single place

    ° It provides the means for printing on another Ethernet segment without allowing normal Windows to broadcast traffic to get across and clutter up the network bandwidth

○ It makes sure that the person printing from his desk on the second floor of the other building doesn't get stuck because the departmental printer on the ground floor of this building has run out of paper and his print job has got redirected to the standby printer

Implicit Class

CUPS also supports the special type of printer class called as **implicit class**. These implicit classes work just like printer classes, but they are created automatically based on the available "printers and printer classes" on the network. CUPS identifies printers with identical configurations intelligently, and has the client machines send their print jobs to the first available printer. If one or more printers go down, the jobs are automatically redirected to the servers that are running, providing fail-safe printing.

We will discuss the implicit class in more detail when we discuss the two server directives "ImplicitClasses" and "ImplicitAnyClasses" in the next chapter.

Managing Printer Classes Through Command-Line

You can perform this task only by using the `lpadmin -c` command. Jobs sent to a printer class are forwarded to the first available printer in the printer class.

Adding a Printer to a Class

You can run the following command with the –p and -c options to add a printer to a class:

```
$sudo lpadmin -p cupsprinter -c cupsclass
```

The above example shows that the printer `cupsprinter` has been added to printer class `cupsclass`:

You can verify whether the printers are in a printer class:

```
$lpstat -c cupsclass
```

Removing a Printer from a Class

You need to run lpadmin command with -p and -r options to remove printer from a class. If all the printers from a class are removed, then that class can get deleted automatically.

```
$sudo lpadmin -p cupsprinter -r cupsclass
```

The above example shows that the printer cupsprinter has been removed from the printer class, cupsclass:

Removing a Class

To remove a class, you can run the lpadmin command with the -x option:

```
$sudo lpadmin -x cupsclass
```

The above command will remove cupsclass

Managing Printer Classes Through CUPS Web Interface

Like printers, and groups of printers, printer classes can also be managed by the CUPS web interface. In the web interface, CUPS displays a tab called **Classes**, which has all the options to manage the printer classes. You can get this tab directly by visiting the following URL:

```
http://localhost:631/classes
```

If no classes are defined, then the screen will appear as follows which shows the search and sorting options:

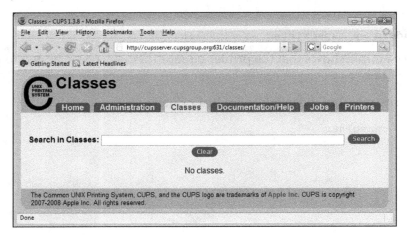

Adding a New Printer Class

A printer class can be added using the **Add Class** option in the **Administration** tab. It is useful to have a helpful description in the **Name** field to identify your class. You can add the additional information regarding the printer class under the **Description** field that would be seen by users when they select this printer class for a job.

The **Location** field can be used to help you group a set of printers logically and thus help you identify different classes. In the following figure, we are adding all black and white printers into one printer class. The **Members** box will be pre-populated with a list of all printers that have been added to CUPS. Select the appropriate printers for your class and it will be ready for use.

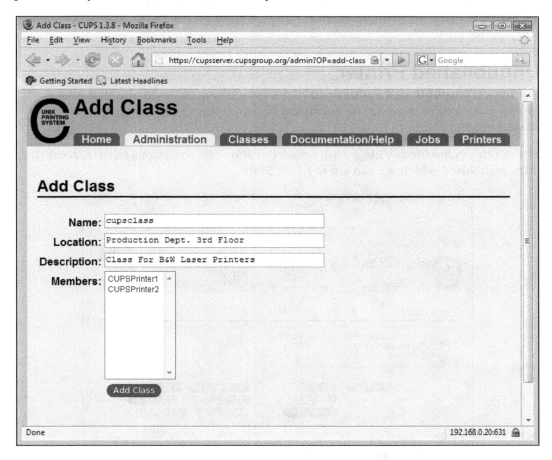

Once your class is added, you can manage it using the **Classes** tab. Most of the options here are quite similar to the ones for managing individual printers, as CUPS treats each class as a single entity

In the **Classes** tab, we can see following options with each printer class:

Stop Class

Clicking on **Stop Class** changes the status of all the printers in that class to "stop". When a class is stopped, this option changes to **Start Class.** This changes the status of all of the printers to "idle". Now, they are once again ready to receive print jobs.

Reject Jobs

Clicking on **Reject jobs** changes the status of all the printers in that class to "reject jobs". When a class is in this state, this option changes to **Accept Jobs** which changes the status of all of the printers to "accept jobs" so that they are once again ready to accept print jobs.

Unpublished Printer

The option **Unpublished Printer** makes the printer unpublished and that means printer is no longer shared. The published printer option activates the printer shared mode.

The default value for any class with respect to above three options is: **idle, accepting jobs, published** which we can see in **Class State**.

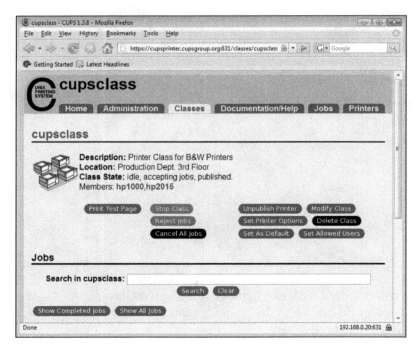

Cancel All Jobs

The option **Cancel All Jobs** will cancel all the jobs of the class.

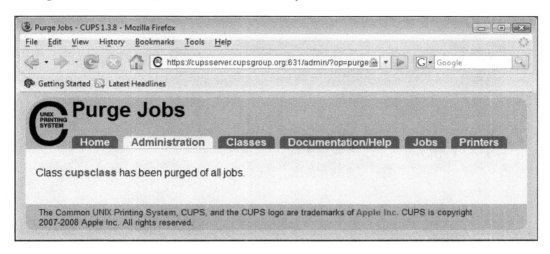

Delete Class

To delete a class, you can use this option. CUPS will show a warning message when a class is deleted.

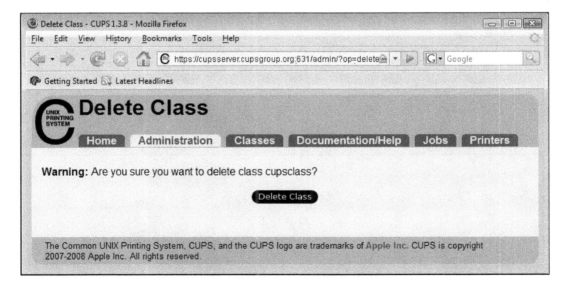

Modifying a Class

To change the properties of a class, you can use the **Modify Class** option. Apart from changing the fields such as **Location** and **Description**, you can also add or remove printer/printers from a printer class.

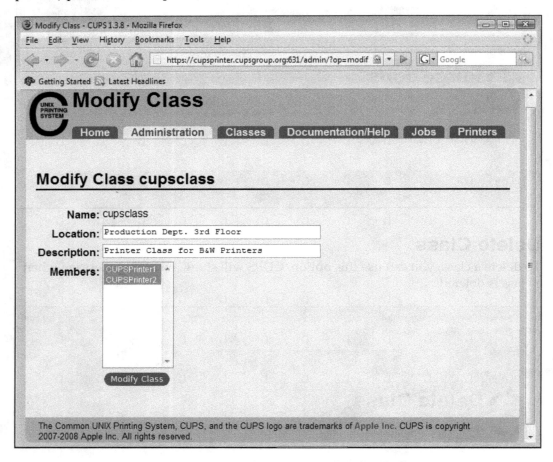

Setting up Printer Options for Class

To set printer options on a printer class, you can use the **Set Printer Options**. There are fewer options that can be set on a class. You can set the options for "Banners" and "Policy" for the printer class.

Banners include the **Starting Banner** and **Ending Banner** (as shown in the following screenshot) for printer. If only one banner file is specified, then it will be printed before the files in the job. If a second banner file is specified, it will be printed after the files in the job.

The available banner pages depend on the local system configuration. CUPS includes the following banner files:

- none — No banner pageIt does not produce a banner page
- classified — A banner page with a **classified** label at the top and bottom
- Confidential — A banner page with a **confidential** label at the top and bottom
- secret — A banner page with a **secret** label at the top and bottom
- standard — A banner page with no label at the top and bottom
- topsecret — A banner page with a **topsecret** label at the top and bottom
- unclassified — A banner page with an **unclassified** label at the top and bottom

Policy includes the options such as **Error Policy** and **Operation Policy** (as shown in the following screenshot) that can be setup on the printer classes.

The **Error Policy** field is used to specify the error policy when there is an error in printer while printing a job. You can use options like **stop-printer**, **retry-job**, **abort-jobs**, and so on within this option.

The **Operation Policy** is the field that denotes the printing policy for the printer. This policy contains information say on whether the printer is set to as default or not.

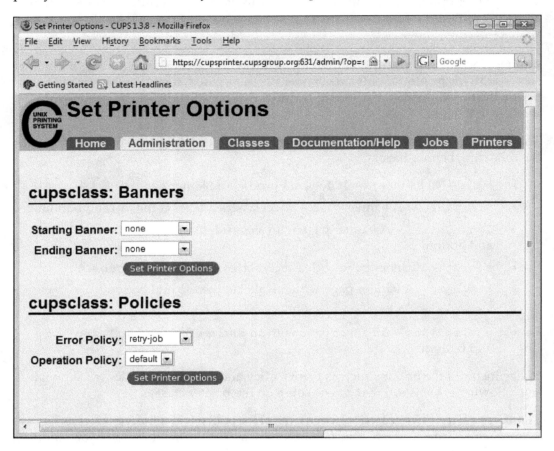

Printing a Test Page for a Printer Class

The **Print Test Page** option prints a test page which can be used to test the functionality of the printer class. If one of the printers is busy or down, the job is sent to another printer in the same printer class.

Setting a Printer Class as Default

The printer class can be set as the default using the option **Set As Default**. When you set up a printer class as the default one, you will get the following note stating that the `lpoptions` setting will override this default setting.

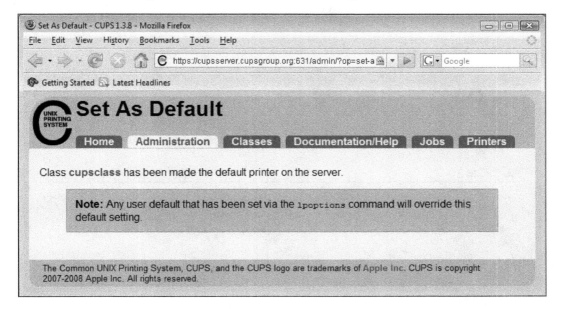

Set Allowed Users

The option **Set Allowed User** is used to restrict users of a printer class. This option will be very useful if someone wants to put usage control on expensive printers, limiting access to the class.

Nested Printer Classes

A printer class can also be included within another printer class, this is called as Nested Printer Class. Let's discuss this with an example. The following screenshot shows the printer class **cupsclass1** which contains a printer **colorprinter** and a printer class **cupsclass**. The. printer class **cupsclass** contains two printers **cupsprinter1** and **cupsprinter2**.

Here one of the members of the printer class, **cupsclass,** is another printer class **cupsclass1**, this is called nesting of classes. This feature can be very useful for you as the administrator can stop individual printers from accepting jobs, forcing users to use the printer classes.

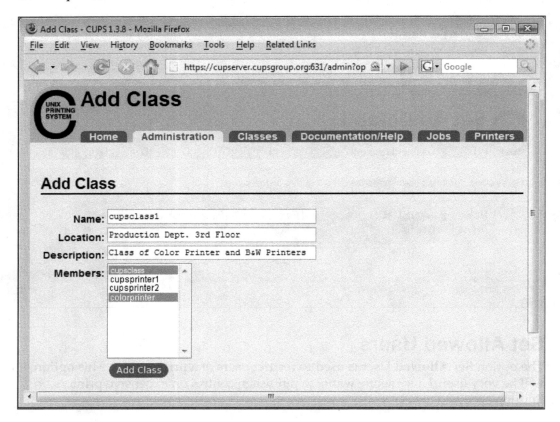

Summary

In this chapter, we have discussed printer classes, their configurations and usage through the command line and web-based interfaces. The advantage of having printer classes is that multiple printers can be used more efficiently (if they are in classes), which means that users can print even if one or more printers in a printer class are down.

5

CUPS Server Management

The initial installation of CUPS allows access only from the host computer, and supports about twenty different print drivers. In this chapter, you will learn to configure the CUPS daemon, so that it is accessible on your whole network. The CUPS server is configured through several files located in the /etc/cups directory. Each of these files uses a format similar to that used by the Apache web server configuration files. This format is:

```
<directive directive-name>
   directive-variables
</directive>
```

System Requirement

Before we start discussing configuration files, let's understand the system requirements for the CUPS server. You should make sure your server meets or exceeds the requirements needed for a printing network of the size you plan on having. This is the URL of the cups website that provides us the details for the system requirements:

```
http://www.cups.org/estimator.php
```

In the left side of the form, you have to submit the number of printers, the size of the network, and the number of jobs. Then, clicking on the **Compute System Requirements** button will give the output as **System Requirements**. The output contains system information such as memory, disk, processors, and some recommended directives which need to be set in the cupsd.conf server configuration file.

Configuration Files

The following are some of the important files, which are normally edited by the CUPS administrator:

Configuration file	Significance
client.conf	This file configures the CUPS client. It contains the directives which provide information about the CUPS server for client machines. We will discuss this briefly in the next chapter, *CUPS Client Setup*.
classes.conf	This file contains information about each printer class. However, it contains only locally defined classes, not remote classes that are created automatically via browsing. Each directive is listed on a line by itself followed by its value.
	It contains the information in plain text that can be modified using your favorite text editor. But it is recommended that you use the lpadmin command, web interface, or any other available GUIs to manage your printer class.
cupsd.conf	This file contains directives that control the manner in which the CUPS server (/usr/sbin/cupsd) operates. You can use lpadmin commands to update this file. We can also use the cupsctl command to do basic changes in this file.
mime.convs	This file is used for raw mode printing, and it contains a list of the standard file conversion filters and their costs. We will discuss this in more detail in Chapter 9 – *File Typing and Filtering*.
mime.types	This file is also used for raw printing, and it has a list of standard file formats and the information needed to recognize them. We will discuss this in detail in Chapter 9.
printers.conf	This file contains information on each printer. Normally, we manipulate this file using the lpadmin command or the web interface.

The **cost** field is used to find the least costly filters to run when converting a job file to a printable format.

The cupsctl command is used to set the basic options of cupsd.conf. If this command is used without any option, it will display the default setting.

You need to restart the CUPS service after one or more of the above files is edited. There are a few ways to do this. One way is to send a HUP signal to the CUPS service, forcing it to restart.

```
$sudo kill -HUP <pid of cups-process>
```

Or

```
$sudo killall -HUP cupsd
```

The service can also be restarted via initialization by adding restart at the end. While installing CUPS, the distribution pack will put this script in init.d with the name cups, but it varies depending on which OS you are running.

For HP-UX:

```
$sudo /sbin/init.d/cups restart
```

For MacOS X:

```
$sudo /System/Library/StartupItems/PrintingServices/PrintingServices
restart
```

For AIX, IRIX, Solaris, and Linux flavors:

```
$sudo /etc/init.d/cups restart
$sudo /etc/software/init.d/cups restart
$sudo /etc/rc.d/init.d/cups restart
```

Classes Directives

As we have seen in the last chapter, the printer class defines the information for a group of printers. This information is placed in the classes.conf file. In this section, we are going to discuss some of the important directives that determine the behavior of the CUPS classes. The printer classes can be managed either directly by editing the classes.conf file or through the command line (lpadmin).

In the following section, we will cover both these methods and explain the following directives in detail:

- Accepting
- Printer
- Class
- DefaultClass
- AllowUser
- DenyUser
- Info
- Location
- JobSheets
- KLimit

- PageLimit
- QuotaPeriod
- State
- StateMessage

Accepting

The `Accepting` directive will start or stop accepting print jobs for the printer group. It defines the initial Boolean value for the `printer-is-accepting-job` attribute that can be set by the accept and reject commands. These `accept` and `reject` commands set the value for these directives to "yes" and "no" respectively.

In the following example, the first command shows that the `cupsclass` class is ready to accept jobs, while the second command shows that it is not accepting jobs:

```
$sudo accept -c cupsclass
$sudo reject -r "This CUPS Class is dowm for repair" -c cupsclass
```

As shown in this example, this directive must appear inside a `Class` or `DefaultClass` directive. We will discuss both these directives later in this section.

```
<Class cupsclass/>
  . . . . . . .
  Accepting no
</Class>
```

 We will try to cover both the ways of setting the value of the directive – via the command line and alternatively by setting the directive values as per the syntax — by editing the above mentioned configuration files directly.

Printer

The `Printer` directive adds a printer to the specified class. It can be added by the `lpadmin -c` command.

 Do not confuse this directive with the one in `printers.conf` as the `Printer` directive in the `printers.conf` defines the information of the printer which has different syntax altogether.

```
$sudo lpadmin -p cupsprinter -c cupsserver
```

We can also perform this action by editing the `class.conf` file. This directive must appear inside a `Class` or `DefaultClass` directive.

```
<Class cupsclass>
   ...
   Printer cupsprinter
</Class>
```

Class

The `Class` directive is used to begin a class definition. It can be added by the `lpadmin -c` command.

$sudo lpadmin -p cupsprinter -c cupsclass

The syntax of the `Class` directive is as follows:

```
<Class cupsclass>
   ...
   Printer cupsprinter
</Class>
```

DefaultClass

The `DefaultClass` directive begins a class definition for the default server destination. It can be added by the `lpadmin -d` command or if already defined, is set as default by the `lpadmin -d` command.

$sudo lpadmin -d cupsclass

The following is the syntax of the directive `DefaultClass` in `classes.conf`:

```
<DefaultClass cupsclass/>
   ...
</DefaultClass>
```

 All the directives of `classes.conf` file must appear inside a `Class` or `DefaultClass` directive.

AllowUser

This directive adds a username to the `requesting-user-name-allowed` attribute, which can be set by the `lpadmin -u` command.

`$sudo lpadmin -p cupsclass -u allow:kajol`

The following example shows that the user `kajol` is allowed to print the jobs for the class this directive is set.

```
<Class cupsclass/>
   .......
   AllowUser kajol
</Class>
```

This directive will not be effective if it is used with `DenyUser` directive. CUPS reads the entire configuration file line by line. So, if in case of both these directives, the directive which is written later in the configuration file will remain effective.

DenyUser

It is very similar to the `AllowUser` directive. It is used to add a username, who should be denied from accessing the CUPS classby using the `lpadmin -u` command.

`$sudo lpadmin -p cupsclass -u deny:hrithik`

The following directive denies user `hrithik` to print new jobs for the class in which it is defined.

```
<Class cupsclass/>
   .......
   DenyUser hrithik
</Class>
```

Info

The `Info` directive defines the string for the `printer-info` attribute, which can be set by the `lpadmin -D` command:

`$sudo lpadmin -p cupsprinter -c cupsclass -D "Class of ColourPrinters"`

The following is an example of the directive when it appears inside a `Class` or `DefaultClass` directive:

```
<Class cupsclass/>
   .......
   Info Class of ColourPrinters
</Class>
```

Location

The `Location` directive defines the string for the `printer-location` attribute, which can be set by the `lpadmin -L` command.

```
$sudo lpadmin -p cupsprinter -c cupsclass -L "Production Dept.3rd Floor"
```

> Do not confuse the `Location` directive with the one in `cupsd.conf` because the two are very different. We will discuss the `cupsd.conf` file later in this chapter.

As shown in the following example, this directive must appear inside a `Class` or `DefaultClass` directive. We can specify the location, for example. "Production Dept.3rd Floor", of the printer using the following example.

```
<Class cupsclass/>
   .......
   Location Production Dept.3rd Floor
</Class>
```

JobSheets

The directive `JobSheets` specifies the default banner pages to print before and after a print job that means these banner pages create a cover sheet for each print job that a printer produces. The following command and example will print only the standard banner at the end of each print job for the class.

```
$sudo lpadmin -p cupsclass -o job-sheets=none,standard
   <Class cupsclass>
      ...
      JobSheets none,standard
   </Class>
```

If only one banner file is specified, it will be printed before the files in the job. If a second banner file is specified, it is printed after the files in the job.

The configuration of the local system is responsible for available banner pages. By default, CUPS includes the following banner files:

- **none** — Does not produce a banner page
- **classified** — A banner page with a **classified** label at the top and bottom
- **confidential** — A banner page with a **confidential** label at the top and bottom
- **secret** — A banner page with a **secret** label at the top and bottom

- **standard** — A banner page with no label at the top and bottom
- **topsecret** — A banner page with a **topsecret** label at the top and bottom
- **unclassified** — A banner page with an **unclassified** label at the top and bottom

You can also create your own banner pages in CUPS that requires you to create banner files supported by CUPS to `/usr/share/cups/banners` as a banner. These banner files can be any printable static file such as PS, PDF, Image/Graphic formats, TIFF, ASCII, and International Text (MIME types as they are defined in `/etc/cups/*.types` on a system). The user can then read this banner once sufficient read privileges have been set. To make your banner effective, you have to restart CUPS scheduler. You can get more information on this on:

```
http://www.cups.org/articles.php?L204+TFAQ+P1+Q
```

KLimit

The `KLimit` directive defines the value of the `job-k-limit` attribute, which can be set by the following command:

```
$ lpadmin -p cupsclass -o job-k-limit=2048

   <Class cupsclass>
     . . .
     KLimit 2048
   </Class>
```

PageLimit

This directive will decide the value of the `job-page-limit` attribute. You can set its value through the following command:

```
$sudo lpadmin -p cupsclass -o job-page-limit=1024
```

Where `1024` is the value set by you.

The same operation can be performed by editing the `class.conf` file in your favorite editor.

```
   <Class cupsclass>
     . . .
     PageLimit 1024
   </Class>
```

QuotaPeriod

The `QuotaPeriod` directive defines the value of the `job-quota-period` attribute, which can be set by the following command:

```
$sudo lpadmin -p cupsclass -o job-quota-limit=604800

   <Class cupsclass>
      . . .
      QuotaPeriod 604800
   </Class>
```

State

The `State` directive defines the initial value of the `printer-state` attribute which sets the initial status of the printer. The following example shows that the initial value of the `cupsclass` has been set to `stopped` status.

```
   <Class cupsclass>
      . . . . . . .
      State stopped
   </Class>
```

You can use `cupsenable` and `cupsdisable` commands to set the current state:

```
$sudo cupsenable cupsclass
$sudo cupsdisable cupsclass
```

StateMessage

The `StateMessage` directive defines the initial string for the `printer-state-message` attribute that means "messages which denote the status of the class".

```
   <Class cupsclass>
      . . . . . . .
      StateMessage Ready to print.
   </Class>
```

The following are some examples of messages that can be used within this directive:

- Connected to `host_name`
- Connecting to `class_queue` on port `port_number`
- Network host `host_name` is busy; will retry in 60 seconds
- Printer busy; will retry in 10 seconds
- Printer is busy; retrying print job

- Print file accepted — job ID id_number.
- Ready to print
- Waiting for the job to complete

Client Directives

The CUPS client applications use the /etc/cups/client.conf file for default settings. This application also looks in the user's home directory for a file called .cupsrc. Each directive is listed on a line by itself followed by its value. It can be edited in your favorite text editor.

The client.conf file contains two directives that determine the behavior of clients:

- ServerName
- Encryption

We will discuss these in detail in the next chapter, *Client Setup*.

ServerName

The ServerName directive specifies and sets the remote server that is to be used for all client operations. This means, it redirects all client requests to the remote server. The default is to use localhost.

```
ServerName cupsserver.cupsexample.com
ServerName 10.20.30.40
```

Encryption

The Encryption directive specifies the default encryption settings for the client. The following are possible values for the Encryption directive:

```
Encryption Never
Encryption IfRequested
Encryption Required
Encryption Always
```

The default setting is IfRequested.

Server Directives

The Common UNIX Printing System server's behavior is configured through the directives contained in the /etc/cups/cupsd.conf file. The CUPS configuration file follows the same syntax as the primary configuration file for the Apache web server. Users familiar with editing Apache's configuration file should feel at ease when editing the CUPS configuration file.

> **Warning**: Prior to editing the configuration file, you should make a copy of the original file and protect it from writing, so you will have the original settings as a reference, and can re-use it as necessary. Copy the /etc/cups/cupsd.conf file and protect it from writing with the following commands:
>
> `$sudo cp /etc/cups/cupsd.conf /etc/cups/cupsd.conf.original`
>
> `$sudo chmod a-w /etc/cups/cupsd.conf.original`
>
> You can then edit the file with your favorite editor.

Editing the cupsd.conf File Via the Web Interface

Type the following URL in your favourite web-browser:

`http://localhost:631/admin`

Click on the **Administration** tab, and then look for the **Server** section in the right-hand column and then click on **Edit Configuration File**.

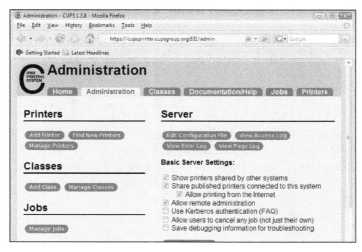

This will open the following window which shows `cupsd.conf` in the editing mode. Once the required changes are made, click on **Save Changes** that will first ask for authorization, and then the CUPS scheduler will start if the correct login information is provided when asked to authenticate. The web interface of CUPS also provides the additional option to use the default configuration file.

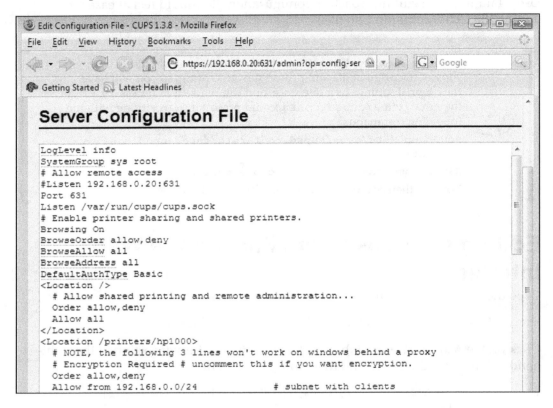

The `cupsd.conf` file describes the behavior of the CUPS Server. It contains multiple directives. We are going to describe some of the important directives in detail.

Important Directives of cupsd.conf

Let's discuss some of the important directives of the `cupsd.conf` file. These directives can be categorized into different categories such as server identity, server options, network options, browsing options, and security options. Let us discuss them in detail.

Server Identity

The directives that describe the identity of the server such as the hostname, administrator, certificate, key, tokens, and so on fall under this category.

ServerAdmin

To configure the email address of the designated administrator of the CUPS server, simply edit the /etc/cups/cupsd.conf configuration file with your preferred text editor, and modify the ServerAdmin line accordingly. For example, if you are the administrator for the CUPS server, and your email address is foo@cupsexample.com, then you would modify the ServerAdmin line to appear as:

```
ServerAdmin foo@cupsexample.com
```

You can also use the cupsctl command with the option directive name=value:

```
$sudo cupsctl ServerAdmin=foo@cupsexample.com
```

> The cupsctl command queries or updates the CUPS server configuration file cupsd.conf. If the directive specified as an option is not present in the existing file, then it will append at the end of the file with the specified value.

ServerName

The host name of the CUPS server can be configured using this directive. For example, if you are the administrator for the CUPS server, and your email address is cupsserver.cupsexample.com, then you would modify the ServerName directive to appear as follows.

```
ServerName cupsserver.cupsexample.com
```

The cupsctl command will perform the same operation as above:

```
$sudo cupsctl ServerName=cupsserver.cupsexample.com
```

Server Options

The Server Options category contains those directives that manage the behaviour of the server.

LogLevel

This directive defines the log behaviours in the `error_log` file. If the value is set to `none`, then it will log nothing. If it is set to `info`, then the server will log general information such as all request and state changes in `error_log`. This is the default value for this directive. The following are the examples of this directive:

```
LogLevel none
LogLevel info
```

If you need to troubleshoot a problem with CUPS, then it should be set to `debug` or `debug2`. The difference between these two directives is that the first one logs the most important logs, while the latter logs everything. These directives will be displayed as:

```
LogLevel debug
LogLevel debug2
```

The value `warn` logs all the errors and the warning, while the `error` will log only errors.

```
LogLevel warn
LogLevel error
```

The other options include `emerg`,`alert`,`crit`, and `notice`. Here are some examples:

```
LogLevel emerg
LogLevel alert
LogLevel crit
LogLevel notice
```

- `emerg` — It logs the emergency conditions that prevent the server from running
- `alert` — It logs the alerts that must be handled immediately
- `crit` — It will log the critical errors that don't prevent the server from running
- `notice` — It logs temporary error conditions

Network Options

The Network Options consist of those directives that provide information about the network.

Listen

The CUPS server installation listens only on the loopback interface at the IP address, 127.0.0.1. In order to instruct the CUPS server to listen on an actual network adapter's IP address, you must specify either a hostname, or the IP address, or optionally, an IP address/port pairing via the addition of a `Listen` directive. For example, if your CUPS server resides on a local network at the IP address 192.168.10.250, and you would like to make it accessible to the other systems on this subnetwork, you would edit the `/etc/cups/cups.d/ports.conf` and add a `Listen` directive, such as:

```
Listen 127.0.0.1:631
```

It will listen to the existing loopback adapter:

```
Listen /var/run/cups/cups.sock
```

Similarly, it will listen to the existing socket:

```
Listen 192.168.10.250:631
```

It will listen on the LAN interface, Port 631 (IPP).

In the above example, you may comment out or remove the reference to the loopback address (127.0.0.1), if you do not wish CUPS to listen on that interface, but would rather have it only listen on the Ethernet interfaces of the Local Area Network (LAN). To enable listening for all network interfaces for which a certain hostname is bound, including the loopback, you could create a `Listen` entry for the hostname `cupsserver` such as:

```
Listen cupsserver:631
```

It will listen on all interfaces or networks for the hostname `cupsserver`.

Port

It specifies the port number on which HTTP requests come. The default value of the CUPS server is 631. You can specify multiple lines of this directive to listen on multiple ports. This directive is similar to `Listen *:nnn` directive, where `nnn` specified the interface:

```
Port 631
Port 80
```

 The `Port` directive will bind both the IPv4 and IPv6 on the systems that support IPv6 addresses.

Browsing Options

This option has all the directives which will give browsing behaviour of the CUPS server. It also gives the information of shared printers on the network.

Browsing

It specifies whether the remote printer browsing is enabled or not. If the value is set to On, then remote printer browsing is enabled, and if it is set to Off, it means browsing for printers is disabled:

```
Browsing On
```

BrowseOrder

This directive describes the order of printer access information; it can either allow access to the printer by default, or deny access.The value will either be allow,deny or deny,allow:

```
BrowseOrder allow,deny
```

BrowseAllow

It specifies the named hosts or addresses from where the printer information can come. The default value for this directive is all:

```
BrowseAllow all
```

The other values that can be set with this directive are: none, hostname, domain name, IP address, or network addresses that are mentioned here:

```
BrowseAllow none
BrowseAllow cupsserver.cupsexample.com
BrowseAllow *.cupsgroup.com
BowseAllow 192.168.10.25
BrowseAllow 192.168.10.0/255.255.255.0
```

The other two options which can be used with this directive are @LOCAL and @IF(name):

```
BrowseAllow @LOCAL
```

The @LOCALaddress broadcasts to all non point-to-point interfaces. For example, if you have a LAN and a dial-up link, @LOCAL would send printer updates to the LAN, but not to the dial-up link:

```
BrowseAllow @IF(eth0)
```

Similarly, the @IF(name) address sends to the named network interface. Interfaces are refreshed automatically (no more than once every 60 seconds), so they can be used on dynamically-configured interfaces, for instance, PPP, 802.11, and so forth.

BrowseDeny

This directive is used to deny incoming printer information packets from the named host or addresses. The options of this directive are similar to the BrowseAllow directive.

BrowseProtocols

It specifies which protocol is used for the browsing. By default, this directive uses two protocols: cups and dns-sd:

```
BrowseProtocols cups dns-sd
```

If the value of this directive is set to none, then it will not use any of the browsing protocol. The value cups denotes that the server uses CUPS browsing. dns-sd, ldap, all, slp, cups which can be set as follows:

```
BrowseProtocols none
BrowseProtocols cups
```

The values dns-sd denotes the DNS service discovery, which is a way of using standard DNS programming interfaces, servers, and packet formats to browse the network for services:

```
BrowseProtocols dns-sd
```

You can get more information on this:

```
http://www.dns-sd.org/
```

The value ldap uses LDAP (Lightweight Directory Access Protocol). CUPS now supports encrypted LDAP:

```
BrowseProtocols ldap
```

If you choose to use SLP (Service Location Protocol), it is strongly recommended that you have at least one SLP Directory Agent (DA) on your network. Otherwise, browsing updates can take several seconds, during which the scheduler will not respond to client requests:

```
BrowseProtocols slp
```

You can also enable every available browsing protocol with the `all` option:

```
BrowseProtocols all
```

BrowseAddress

This directive specifies the broadcast information to be used. By default, the information is not sent. `IP-address`, `@Local`, and `@IF(name)` are the values that can be set with this directive:

```
BrowseAddress 192.168.10.250
BrowseAddress @Local
BrowseAddress @IF(eth1)
```

BrowseShortNames

This directive describes whether or not to use the short name of the remote printers. For example, `printer` instead of `printer@hostname` can be used if this directive is set to `Yes` which is also the default value. This option is ignored if more than one printer exists with the same name.

```
BrowseShortNames Yes
```

Security Options

This section has all the directives that are related to administration, authorization, and security.

SystemGroup

This directive is used to submit the group name for "System" (printer administration) access. The default varies depending on the operating system. It could be "sys", "system", or "root", checked for in that order. For example:

```
SystemGroup sys root
```

AuthType

This directive is used for authorization. The authorizations to be used with this directive are None, Basic, and Digest.

If the directive is set to None, then CUPS doesn't perform any authentication, which means that anonymous access is possible. This is the default value for this directive:

```
AuthType None
```

The authentication type Basic is used to perform basic authentication using OS username and password, on the basis of the /etc/passwd file.

```
AuthType Basic
```

If the value is set to Digest, then it will perform digest authentication using the /etc/passwd.md5 file.

```
AuthType Digest
```

The authentication type BasicDigest is used is used to perform basic authentication using the /etc/passwd.md5 file.

```
AuthType BasicDigest
```

The value Negotiate will perform Kerberos authentication.

```
AuthType Negotiate
```

The AuthType directive must be inside a Location or Limit section, which we will discuss later in this chapter.

While using the Basic, Digest, BasicDigest, or Negotiate options as the authentication type, the clients connecting through localhost interface can also authenticate using certificates.

Location

The Location directive is used to specify authentication options for the HTTP path and access control. This directive has two clauses, one is to start, <Location> and other is to end </Location>.

The `Allow`, `AuthType`, `Deny`, `Encryption`, `Limit`, `LimitExcept`, `Order`, `Require`, and `Satisfy` directives may all appear in between these two clauses. This path is used for getting all operations, for example, `get-printers`, `get-jobs`, and so on:

```
<Location />
  ......
  Allow from none
  Authtype basic
  .....
</Location>
```

This path is used for administration related operations such as `add-printer`, `delete-printer`, `start-printer`, and so on:

```
<Location /admin>
  ...
</Location>
```

The following example specifies the path for accessing the CUPS configuration files such as `cupsd.conf`, `client.conf`, and others:

```
<Location /admin/conf>
  ...
</Location>
```

The following example shows how to get access to the CUPS log files such as `access_log`, `error_log`, `page_log`:

```
<Location /admin/log>
  ...
</Location>
```

The following example specifies the location of all classes:

```
<Location /classes>
  ...
</Location>
```

This directive can also be used to specify the resource information for the `cups` class:

```
<Location /classes/cups>
  ...
</Location>
```

The `Location` directive is used to give information for the path which is related with the jobs related functions such as `hold-job`, `release-job`, and so on:

```
<Location /jobs>
  ...
</Location>
```

You can specify the resource path for the job with the ID (17 in this example):

```
<Location /jobs/17>
  . . .
</Location>
```

The following directive is used to specify the path for all the printers:

```
<Location /printers>
  . . .
</Location>
```

The path for a particular printer can be specified as given here. In this example, cupsprinter denotes the name of the printer:

```
<Location /printers/cupsprinter>
  . . .
</Location>
```

You can specify the PPD file for the printer as mentioned here:

```
<Location /printers/cupsprinter.ppd>
  . . .
</Location>
```

The more specific resources override the less specific ones. So the directives inside the /printers/printername location will override the ones from /printers and similarly, directives inside /printers will override ones from /. None of the directives are inherited.

ImplicitClasses

This directive defines whether to use implicit classes. Printer classes can be specified explicitly in the classes.conf file, based implicitly upon the printers available on the LAN, or both. When ImplicitClasses is set to On, printers on the LAN with the same name (for example, cupsprinter) will be put into a class with the same name. This allows you to setup multiple redundant queues on a LAN without a lot of administrative difficulties. If a user sends a job to cupsprinter, the job will go to the first available queue:

```
ImplicitClasses On
```

This directive is enabled by default, but it gets automatically turned off if the `Browsing` directive is turned off.

ImplicitAnyClasses

This directive controls whether or not to create an implicit class with the name `AnyPrinter` for local and shared printers. When `ImplicitAnyClasses` is set to `On` and a local queue of the same name exists, for example, `cupsprinter` or `cupsprinter@server`, then an implicit class called `Anyprinter` is created instead. When `ImplicitAnyClasses` is `Off`, implicit classes are not created when there is a local queue of the same name. The default setting is `Off`:

```
ImplicitAnyClasses Off
```

 `ImplicitClasses` must be enabled for this directive to have any effect.

If the polling is enabled on the printers on your network, CUPS clients are capable of combining identical printers on different servers into one implicit class. When CUPS creates an implicit class, the client assumes that the printers on each server are actually the same printers being served by queues on more than one server.

For example, if the server at 192.168.1.50 serves a `laserprinter1`, and there is another `laserprinter2` served by the CUPS server at 192.168.2.50, an implicit class named `laserprinter` will be created on a client that uses both printers. If there is also a laserprinter connected directly to the client, CUPS will instead create an implicit class named `anylaserprinter`.

Implicit classes provide redundancy by allowing clients to stop sending print jobs to the first available printer in the implicit class, when one of the servers or printers is unavailable.

The following figure shows an example of an implicit class created when two laser printers are connected to CUPS servers at 192.168.1.50 and 192.168.2.50.

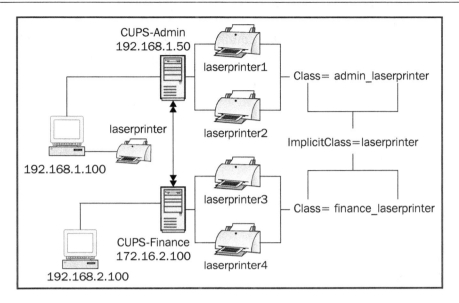

Use of implicit classes allows for simple printer sharing.

In the previous figure, there is no printer connected directly to the workstation at 192.168.2.100. This workstation uses the `laserprinter` implicit class, allowing print jobs to be forwarded to the first available printer on either server.

The workstation at 192.168.1.100 has a direct connection to a `laserprinter`, and this workstation uses the implicit `anylaserprinter`, allowing print jobs to be sent to the local printer, or to the first available printer on either CUPS server.

To see more examples of configuration directives in the CUPS server configuration file, view the associated system manual page by entering the following command at the terminal prompt:

```
$man cupsd.conf
```

Printer Directives

Adding a new printer using the CUPS web interface is very easy. However, you can also configure your printers manually through the configuration files. To do this, you first need to backup your existing configuration, in case you make a mistake and need to restore the original file later.

```
$sudo cp /etc/cups/printers.conf /etc/cups/printers.conf.original
$sudo vi /etc/cups/printers.conf
```

The details for each of the printers is stored in the `printers.conf` file. The configuration directives needed in the configuration file are very simple, and can be explained further by accessing the man page by typing `man printers.conf` at the command prompt. Here are some of the important directives in the `printers.conf` file:

- `Accepting`
- `Printer`
- `DefaultPrinter`
- `DeviceURI`
- `AllowUser`
- `DenyUser`
- `Info`
- `Location`
- `JobSheets`
- `KLimit`
- `PageLimit`
- `QuotaPeriod`
- `State`
- `StateMessage`

Accepting

The `Accepting` directive is used to define the initial Boolean value for the `printer-is-accepting-job` attribute, which can be set by the `accept` and `reject` commands. The `accept` command is used for the parameter value `yes`, while `reject` is used for the value `no`:

```
$sudo accept cupsprinter
$sudo reject cupsprinter
```

This directive must appear inside a `Printer` or `DefaultPrinter` directive:

```
<Printer cupsserver/>
  Accepting no
  ...
</Printer>
```

Printer

The `Printer` directive defines a printer. This directive has two clauses, one is to start `<Printer>` and other is to end `</Printer>`.You can use `lpadmin -p` command to define printer information. You can specify other printer-based directives inside this directive:

```
<Printer cupsserver/>
   . . .
</Printer>
```

DefaultPrinter

The `DefaultPrinter` directive begins a printer definition for the default server destination. It can be added by the `lpadmin` command or if already defined, set as default by the **lpadmin -d** command:

$sudo lpadmin -d cupsprinter

```
<DefaultPrinter cupsprinter/>
   . . .
</Printer>
```

AllowUser

This directive adds a username to the `requesting-user-name-allowed` attribute, which can be set by the `lpadmin -u` command:

$sudo lpadmin -p cupsprinter -u allow:kajol

This directive must appear inside a `Printer` or `DefaultPrinter` directive:

```
<Printer cupsprinter/>
  AllowUser kajol
   . . .
</Printer>
```

DenyUser

It is very similar to the `AllowUser` directive. It is used to add the username of a user who should be denied access to the CUPS class, which can be set using the `lpadmin -u` command:

$sudo lpadmin -p cupsprinter -u deny:hrithik

This directive must appear inside a `Printer` or `DefaultPrinter` directive:

```
<Printer cupsprinter/>
  DenyUser hrithik
  ...
</Printer>
```

DeviceURI

The `DeviceURI` directive defines the value of the `device-uri-attribute` attribute, which can be set by the `lpadmin -v` command:

$sudo lpadmin -p cupsprinter -v socket://foo.bar.com:9100

This directive must appear inside a `Printer` or `DefaultPrinter` directive:

```
<Printer cupsprinter/>
  DeviceURI socket://foo.cupsexample.com:9100
  ...
</Printer>
```

Info

The `Info` directive specifies the string for the `printer-info` attribute, which can be set by the `lpadmin -D` command:

$sudo lpadmin -p cupsprinter -D "ColourNetwork Printer"

This directive must appear inside a `Printer` or `DefaultPrinter` directive:

```
<Printer cupsprinter/>
  Info ColourNetwork Printer
  ...
</Printer>
```

Location

The `Location` directive defines the string for the `printer-location` attribute, which can be set by the `lpadmin -L` command:

$sudo lpadmin -p cupsprinter -L "Production Dept. 3rd Floor"

This directive must appear inside a `Printer` or `DefaultPrinter` directive:

```
<Printer cupsprinter/>
  Location Production Dept. 3rd Floor
  ...
</Printer>
```

Do not confuse the `Location` directive with the one in `cupsd.conf`, which is very different from this, and we have already discussed it in the server directives section.

JobSheets

This directive defines the default banner pages to print before and after a print job.

For example, the following command would produce the same results of a standard banner at the end of each print job for the default class:

```
$sudo lpadmin -p cupsprinter -o job-sheets=none,standard
```

This directive must appear inside a `Printer` or `DefaultPrinter` directive:

```
<Printer cupsprinter/>
  JobSheets none,standard
  ...
</Printer>
```

If only one banner file is specified, it will be printed before the files in the job. If a second banner file is specified, it is printed after the files in the job.

The available banner pages depend on the local system configuration. CUPS includes the following banner files:

- **none** — Do not produce a banner page
- **classified** — A banner page with a **classified** label at the top and bottom
- **confidential** — A banner page with a **confidential** label at the top and bottom
- **secret** — A banner page with a **secret** label at the top and bottom
- **standard** — A banner page with no label at the top and bottom
- **topsecret** — A banner page with a **topsecret** label at the top and bottom
- **unclassified** — A banner page with an **unclassified** label at the top and bottom

KLimit

The `KLimit` directive defines the value of the `job-k-limit` attribute, which can be set by the `lpadmin -o job-k-limit=value`:

```
$sudo lpadmin -p cupsprinter -o job-k-limit=2048
```

This directive must appear inside a `Printer` or `DefaultPrinter` directive:

```
<Printer cupsprinter/>
  KLimit 2048
  . . .
</Printer>
```

PageLimit

The `PageLimit` directive defines the value of the `job-page-limit` attribute, which can be set by the `lpadmin -o job-page-limit=value`:

$sudo lpadmin -p cupsprinter -o job-page-limit=1024

This directive must appear inside a `Printer` or `DefaultPrinter` directive:

```
<Printer cupsprinter/>
  PageLimit 1024
  . . .
</Printer>
```

QuotaPeriod

The `QuotaPeriod` directive defines the value of the `job-quota-period` attribute, which can be set by the `lpadmin -o job-quota-period=value` command:

$ lpadmin -p cupsprinter -o job-quota-limit=604800

This directive must appear inside a `Printer` or `DefaultPrinter` directive:

```
<Printer cupsprinter/>
  QuotaPeriod 604800
  . . .
</Printer>
```

State

The `State` directive defines the initial value of the `printer-state` attribute. The strings `idle` and `stopped` correspond to the IPP enumeration values.

This directive must appear inside a `Printer` or `DefaultPrinter` directive:

```
<Printer cupsprinter/>
  State stopped
  . . .
</Printer>
```

StateMessage

The `StateMessage` directive defines the initial string for the `printer-state-message` attribute.

This directive must appear inside a `Printer` or `DefaultPrinter` directive:

```
<Printer cupsprinter/>
  StateMessage Ready to print.
  ...
</Printer>
```

Here are some more examples:

- Connected to `host_name`
- Connecting to `printer_queue` on port `port_number`
- Network host `host_name` is busy; will retry in 30 seconds
- Printer busy; will retry in 10 seconds
- Printer is busy; retrying print job
- Print file accepted—job ID `id_number`
- Ready to print
- Waiting for job to complete

You can get the information about all the directives of `cupsd.conf` file at:

`http://www.cups.org/documentation.php/ref-cupsd-conf.html`

Concept of Operation Policies

Operation policies are combination of rules used for IPP operations. This feature has been modified to allow you to set rules for each operation or printer. As we discussed,the `Location` directive controls entire server limit, the operation policies on the other hand are used for all IPP requests sent to the CUPS scheduler. These policies are evaluated after `Location` based access control sets and also they control limits on individual printer, task, and service.

These policies are stored in `/etc/cups/cupsd.conf` file in the `Policy` sections. Each policy contains one or more sub directives called `Limit` that lists various operations affected by rules inside it. There should be an alphanumeric name that should be assigned with this directive. You can find an example on this which described the default operation policy in detail at:

`http://www.cups.org/documentation.php/policies.html#LISTING01`

You can also create your own policy if you want to use `Policy` directive, which contains one or more `Limit` directives. The easiest way while creating your own policy is to start with default policy and then make necessary changes inside the copy of it. The policy-name can use the printer's name. The following syntax shows your own policy with one subsection of limit directive for restarting job. If you want any user has right to restart any user's job:

```
<Policy mycupspolicy>
<Limit Restart-Job>
  Order deny,allow
</Limit>
</policy>
```

This `Limit` subsection can use any of these normal limit directives specified at:

http://www.cups.org/documentation.php/policies.html#TABLE02

The following URL shows creating your own policy for computer lab:

http://www.cups.org/documentation.php/policies.html#LISTING02

Once you have created your own policy, you can make it as default one using following directive:

```
DefaultPolicy mycupspolicy
```

You can use the following command to assign this policy to one or more printers. This example shows that the printer cupsprinter is assigned the operation policy mycupspolicy:

```
$sudo lpadmin -p cupsprinter -o printer-op-policy=mycupspolicy
```

Summary

In this chapter, we have discussed system requirements for the CUPS server. We have also discussed server-side configuration and the important files and directives used for that configuration. These configuration files include directives which explain the behavior of printer, class, server, client, and so on.

6
Client Setup

A machine that sends jobs to another machine for printing is called a client and the machine that accepts the job is called a print server. A client can also be a print server if it is directly connected to a printer.

One of the biggest advantages of CUPS is that it allows you to set up a universal print server which can work with almost all printer connection types and most of the printing protocol. The following figure shows that CUPS doesn't only accept print jobs from a local application, but also support the clients working on different platforms. There are various methods to configure clients in CUPS.

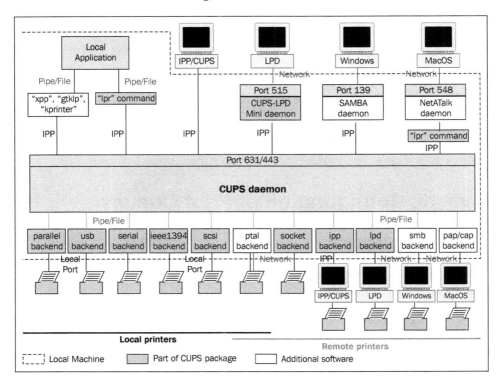

In this section, we are going to check how the CUPS clients working on different platforms can be configured. CUPS can work with different clients such as CUPS/IPP client, LPD client, windows client, Mac client, and so on.

Setting up a CUPS Client

Client set up in CUPS depends on the configuration of two things:

* Print queues
* CUPS Server's communication with clients

Print Queues

You can configure print queues either manually or automatically. Let's discuss this in detail.

Manual Configuration of Print Queues

This is one of the most tedious methods for configuration of client machines. The `lpadmin` command can be used to configure each remote queue manually. The following is an example of:

```
$sudo lpadmin -p cupsprinter -E -v ipp://cupsserver/printers/cupsprinter
```

Here, `cupsprinter` and `cupsserver` are the names of the printer and the hostname, of the print server. You can also use IP address instead of hostname here. This command needs to be repeated for each remote printer being setup.

It is recommended that you configure the CUPS print queues manually, when large numbers of client machines are present. It is very difficult for any administrator to handle numerous client machines. In such a scenario, the clients can be grouped on the basis of subnetting, and printer information can be polled and relayed.

Automatic Configuration of Print Queues

CUPS supports automatic configuration of printers within the same subnet. You don't need to do anything to configure print queues automatically. The CUPS daemon broadcasts information about its printers and classes on the local network. Every client machine on the local network that has a CUPS daemon running picks up these signals and thus, knows which printers and classes are available in the local network. A CUPS client just needs to start its CUPS daemon, and that will make client to have access to all the print queues (on which it is permitted) on the local network.

The broadcasting happens every 30 seconds, so it will take up to 30 seconds for your CUPS client to see all the printers in your local network.

As mentioned earlier, broadcasting works only when the client and server are in the same network. If you want to see the printers and classes available on the other subnets, the directive called `BrowsePoll` is used in `/etc/cups/cupsd.conf`.

The `BrowsePoll` depends on the directive called `BrowseInterval` which again depends on the `BrowseTimeout`.

BrowseTimeout

The timeout (in seconds) for printer or class information is set by the `BrowseTimeout` directive. Once a printer or class times out, it is removed from the list of available destinations. The following is an example that shows that the browse timeout is set to 180 seconds.

```
BrowseTimeout 180
```

BrowseInterval

The maximum amount of time (in seconds) between browsing updates is specified as the `BrowseInterval` directive. If the value is set to 0 seconds, then it disables outgoing browse updates; but it still allows a server to receive printer information from the other hosts.

The value of `BrowseInterval` should always be less than the `BrowseTimeout` value. Otherwise, the printers and classes will disappear from client systems between updates. The following example sets a maximum of 60 seconds for browsing updates.

```
BrowseInterval 60
```

BrowsePoll

The `BrowsePoll` directive polls a server for available printers and classes once every few seconds specified with the `BrowseInterval` directive. To do polling on multiple servers, you can specify multiple instances of the `BrowsePoll` directive. The following example shows two different print servers specified for the polling:

```
BrowsePoll cupsserver.cupsexample.com:631
BrowsePoll 192.168.1.3:631
```

The print server is polled once every 30 seconds, if the value of `BrowseInterval` is set to 0.

BrowseAddress

The `BrowseAddress` directive enables broadcast traffic from the print server, and also specifies an address to send the browsing information. We can also specify multiple `BrowseAddress` directives to send browsing information to different networks or systems. Although the printing information doesn't put much load on network, we can use `BrowseInteral` and `BrowseTimeout` directives to tune the network. The following examples show multiple ways to specify this directive, where @LOCAL denotes all local interfaces across which the information will broadcast and @IF(eth0) will broadcast to the eth0 interface.

```
BrowseAddress @LOCAL
BrowseAddress @IF(eth0)
BrowseAddress 255.255.255.255:631
BrowseAddress 192.168.1.3:631
BrowseAddress cupsserver.cupsexample.com:631
```

CUPS Server's Communication with Clients

The specification for the CUPS server can be identified on the basis of how the server communicates with the client for printing. The following are different situations which we will discuss in detail:

- A single print server
- Multiple print servers across different subnets
- Multiple print servers and clients across different subnets

Single Print Server Configuration

CUPS clients can be used to print without a local spooler, and send all print-jobs to a single print server. But all jobs will fail if the server goes down. You should use this configuration only when it is absolutely necessary.

As discussed in the previous chapter, the default value for the directive `ServerName` is `localhost`. You can override this value by specifying the server hostname or IP address in `/etc/cups/client.conf`. The following example shows that the server name is specified as `cupsserver.cupsexample.com`:

```
ServerName cupsserevr.cupsexample.com
```

Multiple Print Servers Across Different Subnets

In the case where you have multiple print servers spread across different subnets, CUPS can be configured to poll those servers. As discussed earlier, the advantage of polling is that you don't have to configure much on the client side. To enable polling for multiple servers, you have to add multiple entries of the directive BrowsePoll in the CUPS-client configuration file, /etc/cups/client.conf. On the client side, to limit the amount of polling, you have to configure only one client for polling, and the same information can be shared across other clients within the same subnet.

Multiple Print Servers and Clients Across Different Subnets

Since the polling method works on the directive BrowsePoll and as discussed earlier this directive specifies only the information of the print servers. Thus in a setup where you have multiple servers along with multiple clients spread across different subnets, the polling method will not be as effective. In such cases, BrowseRelay, a directive which enables a single client to broadcast (relay) the printing information to a local subnet, can be used.

Let's discuss this feature with an example:

Suppose we have cupsserver1, cupsserver2 and cupsserver3 which are on subnet1, subnet2, and subnet3 respectively, while the client is on subnet4. We want to provide information about the printers across subnet4. In such a case, we need to configure one of the clients in subnet4 with the following directives in the /etc/cups/cupsd.conf file:

[The lines with hash (#) don't perform any operation and must be considered as comments.]

Poll cupsserver1, cupsserver2, and cupsserver3:

```
BrowsePoll cupsserver1
BrowsePoll cupsserver2
BrowsePoll cupsserver3
```

Broadcast (relay) the printers to local subnet (subnet4):

```
BrowseRelay 192.168.1.3 192.168.1.255
```

Here, 192.168.1.3 is the source address—local address for a client machine, which has polled printers' information, and 192.168.1.255 is the destination address—broadcast address for subnet4.

The `BrowseRelay` directive is used to specify the source and destination addresses for relaying browsing information from one host or network to another.

The `BrowseRelay` directive can also be used to broadcast packets from one network to another. So, if client's network interface is attached to all three subnets, then BrowseRelay will look like this:

 # Broadcast the printing information from subnet1, subnet2, and subnet3 to subnet4:

```
BrowseRelay 192.168.1.3 192.168.1.255
BrowseRelay 192.168.2.3 192.168.1.255
BrowseRelay 192.168.3.3 192.168.1.255
```

where 192.168.1.3, 192.168.2.3, and 192.168.3.3 are the addresses of the source interfaces of subnet1, subnet2, and subnet3 respectively and 192.168.1.255 is the destination broadcast address of subnet4.

Relay printer information from polled servers with the following line. This effectively provides access to printers on a WAN for all clients on the LAN(s).

```
BrowseRelay 127.0.0.1 @LOCAL
```

Load Balancing and Failsafe Operation

While broadcasting is used, CUPS clients can automatically merge identical printers spread across multiple servers into a single "implicit class" queue. This is done on the assumption that printers with the same name on multiple print servers are the same, or there are same types of printers.

Let's take an example to explain this scenario:

Suppose you have two laser printers named `cupslaser1` and `cupslaser2` that are configured on two print servers cupsserver1 and cupserver2 respectively. In such a case, an implicit class with the name `cupslaser` will be created automatically on the client.

Now suppose that the client has a local printer with the name `cupslaser` and the directive `ImplicitAnyClass` is set to "On", then the implicit class called `anycupslaser` will be created. As CUPS assumes that the local printer is always available than remote printer, creation of any implicit class is prevented.

 [By default, implicit classes (`ImplicitClasses`) are enabled, and implicit "any" classes (`ImplicitAnyClasses`) are disabled]

The print jobs sent from the CUPS clients will always be available even if one of the servers goes down. Therefore, this automatic switchover function will provide a load-balancing effect and a failsafe operation. .

UNIX/Linux Client

We have already seen two methods for adding a printer for CUPS—through a command line and though a web interface.

You can also add printers through various utilities provided by GNOME, KDE, and others. The following is an example of adding a printer through the GNOME interface.

Adding a Printer

To add printer in GNOME: go to the **Desktop** menu, select the **Administration** tab and then the **Printing** option as mentioned in the following screenshot:

Once it opens, you can see all the available printers. To add a new printer, select menu **Printer** and click on **Add Printer** This will open a new screen as displayed in the following screenshot:

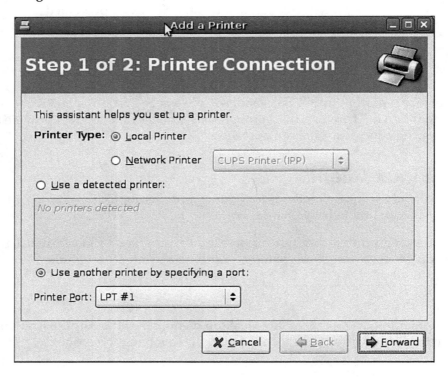

In the above screen, select the **Network Printer** option, and then select **CUPS Printer** and enter the URI. Now click on **Forward**.

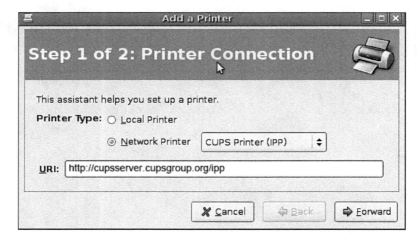

Select your printer manufacturer and model, or install the printer drivers and click on **Apply**.

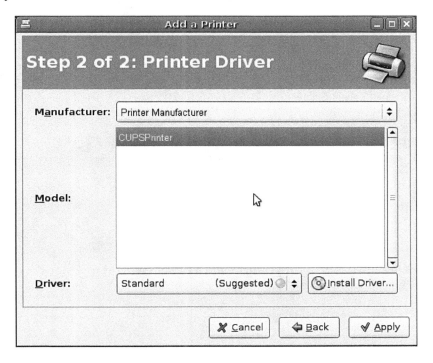

After finishing the setup, you should see something similar to the following screen. Now your printer is ready for printing:

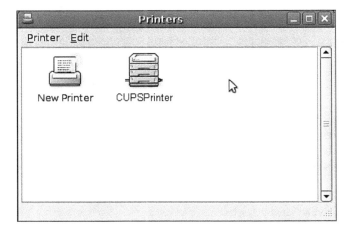

LPD Clients

LPD stands for Line Printer Daemon. It is a printer protocol that uses TCP/IP to establish connections between the print servers and clients in a network.

Unlike CUPS clients, LPD clients cannot do all printing operations because LPD has limited functionality support in CUPS. Even though you can perform normal print functions such as print file, check queue status list and so on., the automatic client configuration and other printer options are not supported by the LPD protocol. It must be configured manually.

The program, cups-lpd, communicates between CUPS and LPD clients. It can be configured with either of these two programs:

- xinetd
- inetd

xinetd

If you are using the xinetd program, create a file named /etc/xinetd.d/lpd containing the following lines:

```
service lpd
{
socket_type = stream
protocol = tcp
wait = no
user = lp
group = sys
server = /usr/lib/cups/daemon/cups-lpd
server_args = -o document-format=application/octet-stream
passenv =
env = TMPDIR=/var/spool/cups/tmp
disable = no
}
```

This information is automatically read by the xinetd program, and then this program also enables LPD printing support. A service with any of the following commands must be started to activate the changes:

```
$sudo /etc/init.d/xinetd restart

$sudo /etc/software/init.d/xinetd restart

$sudo /etc/rc.d/init.d/xinetd restart
```

You can then check the status of the `xientd` using the following commands:

```
$sudo /etc/init.d/xinetd status
```

Or

```
$sudo ps -ax | grep xinetd
```

inetd

If you are using the `inetd` program, the following line should be added in the `/etc/inetd.conf` file. This will enable LPD support on your system:

```
lpd stream tcp nowait lp /usr/lib/cups/daemon/cups-lpd cups-lpd
```

 The path to `cups-lpd` may vary depending upon your installation.

Once the above line is added, the system should be rebooted or the HUP signal should be sent:

```
$sudo killall -HUP inetd
```

Or

```
$sudo kill -HUP pid
```

Warning

 The program `cups-lpd` doesn't have any built-in access control feature based on `cupsd.conf` settings. It also doesn't support TCP wrappers; therefore, `cups-lpd` will allow any client on the network or even anyone on the Internet depending on your network setup to the print server.

While `xinetd` has a built-in access control support, you can use the TCP wrappers package with `inetd` to limit access to only those computers that should be able to print through the server.

Windows Clients

The versions of Windows prior to 2000 did not have the capability to network natively with IPP-based printers. However, Windows 2000 and later versions do have this capability. Therefore, to add a CUPS printer in these versions of Windows is quite easy. You can use **Add Printer Wizard**. You can start adding a printer by clicking on **Next**.

This will open a new window as shown in the following screenshot and it will ask you about the type of printer you have attached. To set up a printer for CUPS, you need to select the radio button showing **A network printer, or a printer attached to another computer** option and then click on **Next.**

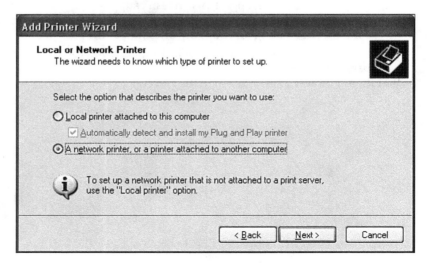

In the next window, select the radio button with the option **Connect to a printer on the Internet or on a home or office network:** and type the URL for the print queue. It will look like this:

```
http://cupsserver-name-or-ip:631/printers/printername
```

You can then click on **Next** to proceed further.

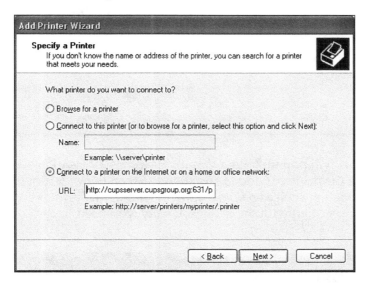

In the resulting windows, make selections based on the make and model of the printer. Select the printer manufacturer in the left scrolling list, and select the printer model in the right list. If you have a disk with the printer drivers from the manufacturer of the printer you are adding, use the option **Have Disk** and then click on **OK**.

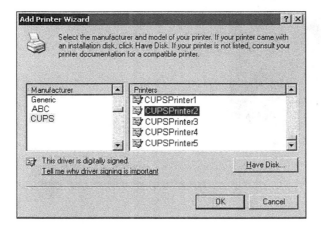

The next window shows the options for the default printer. If you want to run the printer as the default one, select the radio button showing **Yes** option and then click on **Next**.

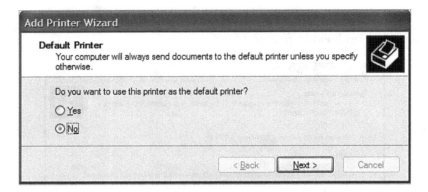

The final window will pop up telling you if you were successful in adding the printer or not. If the printer is added successfully, then the wizard will show some important information such as name, location, whether the printer is default and if any comment is specified with the printer. Finally, you need to click on **Finish** to close the wizard.

Printing with Samba

For printing with Windows clients, we can also use Samba, which is an open source suite that has the capability of providing the file and print services for Windows. It is licensed under GNUL/GPL.The current version of Samba is 3.2.0 which can be downloaded from:

```
http://www.samba.org/
```

You can check whether Samba is already installed or not using the following command:

```
$sudo rpm -qa | grep smb
```

Or

```
$sudo /etc/rc.d/init.d/smb status
```

Now, to check whether Samba is linked against the CUPS library, we can use the `ldd` command.

```
$sudo ldd 'which smbd'
    libssl.so.0.9.6 => /usr/lib/libssl.so.0.9.6 (0x4002d000)
    libcrypto.so.0.9.6 => /usr/lib/libcrypto.so.0.9.6 (0x4005a000)
    libcups.so.2 => /usr/lib/libcups.so.2 (0x40123000)
```

If `libcups` is listed as shown in this example, then Samba is working fine. If not, you need to get CUPS-enabled packages of Samba from distribution or compile Samba from source. If Samba is compiled from the source, then you need to have the header/development package of the CUPS library (`libcups-devel`, `cupsys-dev`, or similar) installed.

You also need to make sure that the name of any printer doesn't exceed 12 characters. If any queue name is longer, then edit the `/etc/cups/printers.conf` file and modify the queue name.

Also, we need to make sure that all the Windows clients or networks consisting of the Windows client should allow access to CUPS. This can be done by adding a line in the `/etc/cups/cupsd.conf` file. The following example shows that the printing is allowed from a windows client with the IP address 192.168.1.3:

```
Allow From 192.168.1.3
```

The above change will be activated after restarting the service:

```
$sudo service cupsd restart
```

Or

```
$sudo killall -HUP cupsd
```

After doing this, we need to modify the file /etc/samba/smb.conf:

```
[global]
load printers = yes
printing = cups
printcap name = cups

printer admin = @cupsadmin
[printers]
comment = All Printers
path = /var/spool/samba
browseable = no
public = yes
guest ok = yes
writable = no
printable = yes
printer admin = root, @cupsadmin

[drivers$]
comment = Windows Printer Driver Download Area
path = /usr/share/cups/windrivers
browseable = yes
guest ok = yes
read only = yes
write list = root, @cupsadmin
```

In the above configuration file, the two lines which are very important are:

- printing = cups
- printcapname = cups

This makes Samba use the functions of the CUPS library to access printers. You also need to check whether the spool directory for Samba mentioned in path = /var/spool/samba is created. If not, we can create it manually using the following command:

```
$sudo mkdir /var/spool/samba
```

The directory should have the necessary write permission, so that Windows client can write to it:

```
$sudo chmod 777 /var/spool/samba
```

The group with the name `cupsadmin`, which should have Samba Printing Administration rights, should also be created. You should make sure that the any other directory in the above scenario (for example `/usr/share/cups/windrivers`) that has a reference should be created with the necessary permission.

Now, you need to create a Samba account for "root" and all the users of the `cupsadmin` group with the command `smbpasswd`.

```
$sudo smbpasswd -a root
```

The `[drivers$]` section defines a file share where Windows printer drivers are located so that Windows clients can download them automatically.

 Check whether there is a line `use client driver = yes` (probably in the `[printers]` section) in the `/etc/samba/smb.conf` file. If it is present, comment out this line by putting a # at the start of the line, as it prevents the automatic download of the PostScript driver from your Samba server.

The listed configuration makes all printers known to the local CUPS daemon, being shared via Samba. This means that they will all be detected in the **Network Neighborhood** or in the **Add Printer Wizard** under Windows. To print with these printers from the Windows client, either the user should use Windows drivers that come with the printers and set up queues on each client (Client Based Queue) or upload the drivers to the Samba server (Sever Based Queue) onto `/usr/share/cups/windrivers` and make it available for all the Windows clients. But before this, the Windows drivers should be downloaded.

You can download Windows drivers from following site:

`http://www.cups.org/windows/index.php`

These drivers are preferred over the Adobe drivers because they support the following additional features:

- A much more accurate page accounting
- Banner pages and page labels on all printers
- Setting up of a number of jobs IPP attributes (such as job priority, page label, and job billing)

Once you have extracted the driver files, copy them to the /usr/share/cups/ drivers directory exactly as mentioned here:

```
cups6.inf
cups6.inf
cupsps6.dll
cupsui6.dll
```

You also need to copy some of these files your Windows machine to the above machine directory:

```
ps5ui.dll
pscript.hlp
pscript.ntf
pscript5.dll
```

You can also download Adobe printer drivers from the Adobe web site:

```
http://www.adobe.com/
```

If you want to use Adobe print drivers, then it needs to be extracted using an unzip program. Once the extraction is done, we can see the following files. Some of the files need to be renamed to ensure that all the file names are in uppercase.

 The case is significant, so make sure that you use the uppercase filenames shown above, otherwise cupsaddsmb will fail to export the drivers.

```
ADFONTS.MFM
ADOBEPS4.DRV
ADOBEPS4.HLP
ADOBEPS5.DLL
ADOBEPSU.DLL
ADOBEPSU.HLP
DEFPRTR2.PPD
ICONLIB.DLL
PSMON.DLL
```

You can upload/export the Windows drivers using the cupsaddsmb command:

```
$sudo cupsaddsmb -U root cupsprinter1 ... cupsprinterN
```

If cupaddsmb runs with the -a option, it will upload/export all the printer drivers:

```
$sudo cupsaddsmb -U root -a
```

The CUPS printer driver is available from the CUPS download site at:
`http://www.cups.org/windows/software.php`

Currently only Windows NT, 2000, and XP are supported by the CUPS drivers. You will also need to get the respective part of the Adobe driver if you need to support Windows 95, 98, and ME clients.

You will need to provide the Samba password if asked. You should also configure CUPS to allow printing in a RAW format from the Windows clients. **For that, we must uncomment the line related to the** `octet-stream` **file:**

In the `/etc/cups/mime.convs` file, uncomment the following line:

```
application/octet-stream application/vnd.cups-raw  0 -
```

In the file `/etc/cups/mime.types`, the following should be uncommented,

```
application/octet-stream
```

We will discuss these two files in the chapter, *File Typing and Filtering* in detail. The CUPS service needs to be restarted to activate these changes.

Printing with Other Systems

CUPS supports printing using other systems:

- Printing with LPD Servers (lpd)
- Printing with Mac OS X 10.2 or later
- Printing with Windows Servers (smb)

Printing with LPD Servers (lpd)

As discussed in Chapter 3, CUPS supports various protocols as backends that also include a TCP/IP based `lpd`, which supports LPD servers and printers. The LPD printing normally happens over port 515. You can specify the device URIs to print to LPD servers as follows:

```
lpd://cupsserver-name-or-ip
```

The LPD backend supports several options which are included in the device URI, such as:

```
lpd://cupsserver/name?option1=value1+option2=value2+...+optionN=
                                                            valueN
```

The following table describes the options and their values that are supported by LPD:

Option	Option=Value	Description
banner	banner=off banner=no banner=false	When any of these options are used, it means that there is no request for a LPD banner page for the job. This is also a default option.
	banner=on banner=yes banner=true	Any of these options can be used to request a LPD banner page for the job.
	format=c	It specifies that the print data is a CIF file.
	format=d	It specifies that the print data is a DVI file.
	format=f	It specifies that the print data is a plain text file.
	format=g	It specifies that the print data is a Berkeley plot file.
	format=l	It specifies that the print data is a raw (preformatted) print file and it is also a default option.
	format=n	This option specifies that the print data is a ditroff file.
format: The option specifies the LPD format code of the print job.	format=o	It specifies that the print data is a PostScript file.
	format=p	It specifies that the print data is a plain text file that should be "pretty" printed with a header and footer.
	format=r	This option specifies that the print data is a FORTRAN carriage control file.
	format=t	It specifies that the print data is a troff Graphic Systems C/A/T phototypesetter file.
	format=v	It specifies that the print data is a Sun raster file.
manual_copies	manual_copies=off manual_copies=no manual_copies=false	Any of these options is used to specify that the backend should not send multiple copies of a print job in the print data file.
	manual_copies=on manual_copies=yes manual_copies=true	Any of these options are used to specify that the backend should send multiple copies of a print job in the print data file to print more than one copy. This is also the default option.

Option	Option=Value	Description
order	order=control,data	It specifies that the LPD control file should be sent before the print data file. This is also the default option.
	order=data,control	This option specifies that the print data file should be sent before the LPD control file.
	reserve=off reserve=no reserve=false	The option specifies that the backend should not reserve a privileged source port as required by RFC 1179.
reverse	reserve=on reserve=yes reserve=true reserve=rfc1179	It specifies that the backend should reserve a privileges source port from 721 to 731 inclusive as required by RFC. 1179. This option may cause reduced. printing performance when more than 11 LPD printers are defined on the server due to port contention issues.
	reserve=any	The option specifies that the backend should reserve a privileges source port from 1 to 1023 inclusive. This often works with LPD implementations that require a privileged source port, but do not limit it to the range defined by RFC 1179, allowing more printers to be active at the same time.It is also the default option.
sanitize_title	sanitize_title=off sanitize_title=no sanitize_title=false	Any of these options can be used to specify that the title string should not be restricted to ASCII characters. It is the default option on Mac OS X.
	sanitize_title=on sanitize_title=yes sanitize_title=true	Any of these options can be used to specify that the title string should be restricted to ASCII characters. It is the default option on all OS except for Mac OS X.
timeout	timeout=N	It specifies the response timeout for all LPD commands and transactions in seconds. The default value for this option is 300 seconds.
contimeout	contimeout= seconds	It specifies the number of seconds to wait for the connection to the server to be complete.

The Request for Comment (RFC) 1179 is about the line Printing Daemon. You can find more information about it at:

`http://www.rfc.net/rfc1179.html`

Printing with Mac OS X 10.2 or later

Mac OS X 10.2 and later includes CUPS as part of the standard printing subsystem. You just need to enable the sharing for the printers to allow the CUPS client to print from the Mac OS X.

Mac OS X supports PPD files for PostScript printers; and for non PostScript Printers, you need to download ESP Gostscript, and/or GIMP-Print drivers, which can be downloaded from:

`http://gimp-print.sourceforge.net/MacOSX.php3`

 It also, with the version 10.2.0 of Mac OS X, all CUPS printers are directly available to all Mac clients automatically.

Printing with Windows Servers (smb)

CUPS can print to Windows server in two different ways:

- lpd
- Samba

LPD

LPD is a communication protocol, which is recognised as "lpd" on print server which is running CUPS and "TCP/IP Printer Service" on Micosoft Windows systems. The following URL will give you tips for enabling this service in detail:

`http://gentoo-wiki.com/HOWTO_print_winserver`

In Microsoft Windows, the LPD service comes with the name **TCP/IP Printing Services**. This service can be enabled by the following steps:

1. Go to **Control Panel**
2. Select **Administrative Tools,** open **Services**
3. Select **TCP/IP Printing Services** service
4. Click on the **Start** button

You can also use Windows printer as "Raw" printer in CUPS as following:

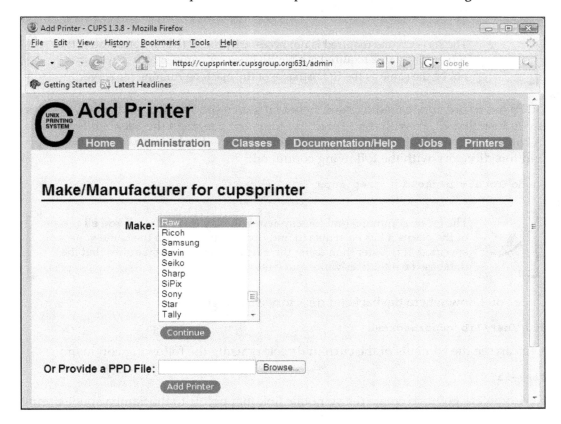

Samba

Samba servers provide the utility command called `smbclient`. You can check whether Samba is working with one of the following commands:

`$sudo smbclient -U Domain/Username -L //winserver`

If the shared printer is not on a domain:

`$sudo smbclient -L //winserver`

The `smbclient` will ask you to enter your password, upon pressing return. If you are on a domain, enter the password that corresponds to your username, otherwise pressing enter should suffice.

You can also find out the name of the server by browsing a network via "My Network Places" or Network Neighborhood.

 The server name required is not necessarily the IP (DNS) hostname of the server. The name required is a NetBIOS server name, which may or may not be the same as the IP hostname of the machine running the server.

CUPS has a directory called `backend` where it stores spooler files for various devices. If you installed CUPS with the `--prefix=/usr` option, then the backbends will be in `/usr/lib/cups/backend`. If you keep your `locate` database up to date, we can find this directory with the following command:

`$sudo locate backend | grep cups`

 The locate command on Linux system will very **quickly** tell you all of the places it has been able to find (locate) the file with the name you specified. It is faster than using the **find** command, but requires that the database be built in advance and be up to date.

Once you know where the backend directory is, change it to:

`$cd /usr/lib/cups/backend`

You can see the contents of the current directory using the following command:

`$ls -la`

Here, you are going to create the symbolic link that points to the Samba spooler wing using the following command:

`$ln -s 'which smbspool' smb`

 Smbspool must be enclosed in back ticks, not single quotes. The back ticks will execute the command within, and use the result in the `ln` command. It is equivalent to executing the command:

`$sudo ln -s /usr/bin/smbspool smb`

Now that you have made this link to the Samba spooler, you have to restart CUPS, so that you can be sure that the change you made will take effect:

`$sudo /etc/rc.d/init.d/cups restart`

Once CUPS has been restarted, we can proceed to adding and configuring the printer. There are a few possible ways to do this:

- Configuring printer using the Command Line Interface (lpadmin)
- Web Interface

Configuring Printer using the Command Line Interface (lpadmin)

The `lpadmin` command is used to add the printer. You need to make sure that you have the correct ppd file for our printer model. If you are not sure, you can download the correct ppd from the various sources which we have already discussed. You can also check the `/usr/share/cups/model` directory to find the ppd file that can work with our printer.

The `lpadmin` command is used to add a Samba printer is as follows:

```
$sudo lpadmin -p cupsprinter -v smb://username:password@cupsserver/\
   printer -P /path/to/printermodel.ppd
```

The `cupsprinter` that follows the `-p` is the name by which we refer to the printer.

If the requested printer isn't on a domain, but shared and attached directly to a machine, the Username: Password portion of the device URI will be a username and password to an account that has access to the shared printer.

If you receive an **error-client-not-possible** message, then it is likely that there is a typo in the URI or that the symbolic link to the smbspool is missing or pointing to the wrong location.

After adding the printer, it needs to be enabled before it can accept any print jobs. The default status of a printer added with the above `lpadmin` command is **stopped, rejecting jobs**. Use the following commands `cupsenable` and `accept` to start the printer, and tell it to accept jobs:

```
$sudo cupsenable cupsprinter
```

```
$sudo accept cupsprinter
```

You can check the status of all the printers with the following command:

```
$lpstat -a
```

It should show that the printer is accepting jobs. At this point, try to print using the `lpr` command. If that doesn't work, try restarting CUPS.

If the problem continues, set the drective `LogLevel` to debug in the `cupsd.conf` file. It should be in the `/etc/cups/` directory. After doing this, restart CUPS, and read the `/var/log/cups/error_log` file.

The log file can usually explain the problem you are having. We will discuss this in detail in the Chapter 8—*Monitoring CUPS* where we will discuss monitoring techniques.

Configuring Printer using the Web-Based Interface

As discussed in Chapter 3, you can use the **Add Printer** wizard of CUPS web interface. This wizard asks for the printer name, location, and description where only the printer name is mandatory. It then asks the make and model of the ppd where you can either select this operation from available database of drivers or you can provide the path of the ppd if available. Then you need to select the device URI for the printer. The following are some examples of the device URI when the printer is added using the Samba:

```
smb://sambaserver/share
smb://user:pass@workgroup/sambaserver/share
smb://user:pass@sambaserver/share
smb://workgroup/sambaserver/share
```

The user:pass string is required if the NT authentication method is enabled for printing or sharing. Also, the workgroup should be specified only when the network contains several workgroups.

Summary

In this chapter, we have discussed integration of the CUPS systems with different clients and systems. Today, support for IPP has made this integration really easy. Also, CUPS provides strong support for other protocols, and this makes it easy for CUPS to work with other systems.

7
Quota Management

The CUPS printing system can manage print jobs based on quotas. Although the quota management in CUPS is not as full-featured as it could be, we will discuss both it's strengths and weaknesses in this chapter.

Setting up Quota in CUPS

As we have discussed in the earlier chapters, quotas can be set with the -o (option) parameter while installing a printer, or later with the lpadmin command for an already existing printer. Quotas can be setup with the following options:

- CUPS supports the page-count and file size-based quotas for each printer.

- Quotas are calculated for each user individually. Thus a single set of limits applies to all users for the concerned printer.

- Quotas can include banner pages (if those are used). It means that we can put a limit on every user to print a certain number of pages (say 10 pages) per day on an expensive printer.

- Options such as **job-k-limit**, **job-page-limit**, and **job-quota-period** are very important for defining quota while setting up a printer.

- **job-k-limit** has a default value 0, which specifies that there is no limit.

- **job-page-limit** has a default value 0, which specifies that there is no limit.

- **job-quota-period** sets a time interval for quota computing. The default value of 0 for **job-quota-period** specifies that the limits apply to all the jobs that have been printed by a user that are still known to the system.

- The intervals are determined in seconds; so a day is 60*60*24=86,400, a week is 60*60*24*7=604,800, and a month is 60*60*24*30=2,592,000 seconds.

job-k-limit

The **job-k-limit** option specifies the maximum number of kilobytes that may be printed by a user, including banner files.

```
$sudo lpadmin -p cupsprinter -o job-k-limit=1024
```

The above example shows the limit for each job is set to 1MB.

job-page-limit

The **job-page-limit** option specifies the maximum number of pages that may be printed by a user, including banner files. In the following example, the page-limit for each job is 100 pages:

```
$sudo lpadmin -p cupsprinter -o job-page-limit=100
```

job-quota-period

The **job-quota-period** option specifies the time period used for quota calculations, in seconds. The default value of 0 specifies that the limits apply to all the jobs that have been printed by all authorized users who have their user accounts set up in CUPS. In the following example, the limit is set to one week for the job-quota-period:

$sudo lpadmin -p cupsprinter -o job-quota-period=604800

You can also create the policy containing a combination of the above parameters. The following are common examples of setting up quota limits:

```
$sudo lpadmin -p cupsprinter -o job-quota-period=604800 -o job-k-\
    limit=1024
```

This sets a total weekly file size limit of 1 MB for each user when printing to the printer cupsprinter.

```
$sudo lpadmin -p cupsprinter -o job-quota-period=604800 -o job-page-\
    limit=100
```

This example sets a limit for each user based on the number of pages they print a week. If the user tries to print more than 100 pages in a week, the extra pages will be denied by CUPS.

```
$sudo lpadmin -p cupsprinter -o job-quota-period=604800 -o job-k-\
    limit=1024 -o job-page-limit=100
```

This command combines the two previous quota limits. It restricts users to 100 pages or 1 MB of printed material per week. When either of the limits is reached, the user won't be able to print any more for that week.

User Restrictions

You can apply the quota policies mentioned above to individual users (instead of all users). The `-u` option of the `lpadmin` command controls which users can print to a printer. The default configuration allows all users to print to a printer:

```
$sudo lpadmin -p cupsprinter -u allow:all
```

CUPS supports `allow` and `deny` lists so that you can specify a list of users who are allowed to print or not allowed to print. This can be done by specifying options such as `-u allow: user1, user2...` as well as the `-u deny: user1, user2...`

The following example will elaborate this idea:

```
$sudo lpadmin -p cupsprinter -o job-quota-period=604800 \
      -o job-k-limit=1024 -o job-page-limit=100 \
      -v file:/dev/null -u deny:root,kajol -E \
      -L "Printer on 2nd Floor" \
      -D "This example shows how quotas and user-ACLs work" \
      -P /etc/cups/ppd/P420.ppd
```

The above command not only applies a quota for `job-quota-perod`, `job-k-limit`, and `job-page-limit`, but also restricts users. In the given command, users `root` and `kajol` are excluded with this quota policy.

The example above would work fine. However, it would be ideal (but not required) to have the entire command on a single line without the backslashes (\).

The above quota policy can also be applied by adding the following entry into the `/etc/cups/printers.conf`:

```
<Printer cupsprinter>
   Info This example shows how quotas and user-ACLs work
   Location Printer on 2nd Floor
   DeviceURI file:/dev/null
   State Idle
   Accepting Yes
   JobSheets none none
   QuotaPeriod 604800
```

```
        PageLimit 100
        KLimit 1024
        DenyUser root
        DenyUser kajol
    </Printer>
```

If you accidentally specify illegal values when you are entering the command, only those options with legal values will be applied. For example, if both the options `-u allow:` and the `-u deny:` are mentioned within the same command line (which is illegal), the command still behaves safely in the sense that only **the last given option will actually be used as it overrides the first one.**

```
$sudo lpadmin -p cupsprinter -o job-quota-period=604800 -o job-k-\
    limit=1024 -o job-page-limit=100 -v file:/dev/null \
    -u deny:root,kajol -u allow:hritik,aamir -E  \
    -L "Printer on 2nd Floor" \
    -D "This example shows how quotas and user-ACLs work"\
    -P /etc/cups/ppd/P420.ppd
```

The above command will ignore the value specified with the `-u deny:`. This means that the above quota policy will be applied to the users `hritik` and `aamir` only. The final entry of the above command in the `/etc/cups/printers.conf` file will look like this:

```
    <Printer cupsprinter>
        Info This example shows how quotas and user-ACLs work
        Location Printer on 2nd Floor
        DeviceURI file:/dev/null
        State Idle
        Accepting Yes
        JobSheets none none
        QuotaPeriod 604800
        PageLimit 100
        KLimit 1024
        AllowUser hritik
        AllowUser aamir
    </Printer>
```

To turn off all quotas again for a given printer, use a `job-k-limit` of 0, and a `job-page-limit` of 0. For example, issue the following command with `cupsprinter` as the printer where you want to turn the quotas off:

```
$sudo lpadmin -p cupsprinter -o job-k-limit=0 -o job-page-limit=0
```

Error Messages

If a user reaches his quota limit, he will receive an error message, **client-error-not-possible**, after giving the print command.

Correct and Incorrect Accounting

While printing in CUPS, the count should be tracked correctly. The filter `pstops` will give the correct count value when the `printfile` passes through it. Without this filtering, CUPS will use a dummy count of "one". Some print files (for example image files) do not pass through this filter. But that doesn't affect the accounting as most of the image files are one page jobs. This also means that proprietary drivers for the target printer running on the client computers and CUPS/Samba, which then `spool` these files as "raw" (leaving them untouched, not filtering them), will be counted as a one page file as well. In such a scenario, you need to send PostScript from the clients (that is, run a PostScript driver on the client machine to have proper accounting of the correct number of pages). If the printer is a non-PostScript model, you need to let CUPS convert the file to a print-ready format for the target printer.

Overview of the page_log file

You will find the following items in the CUPS `page_log` file for each page in a job:

- Printer name: The **printer** field contains the name of the printer that prints the page. If a job is sent to a printer class, this field will contain the name of the actual printer that was assigned the job.

- User name: The **user** field contains the name of the user who submitted the print job for printing. The user's name is obtained from the IPP `requesting-user-name` attribute.

- Job ID: The **job-id** field contains the job number of the page being printed. The job numbers are reset to "1" whenever the CUPS server is started. So, it is recommended that you don't depend on this number being unique.

- Time of printing: The **date-time** field contains the date and time of request in local time when the page started printing, and its format is: [DD/MMM/YYYY: HH:MM:SS+ZZZZ], where:

    ○ DD—The day of the month between 01 and 31

    ○ MMM—Month name in 3 characters.(examples, Jan, Feb, and so on)

    ○ YYYY—A four-digit year

- ○ HH — Number of complete hours that have passed since midnight (00-24) and if the hour value is 24, then the minute and second values must be zero
- ○ MM — Number of complete minutes that have passed since the start of the hour (00-59)
- ○ SS — Number of complete seconds since the start of the minute (00-60)
- ○ ZZZZ — time zone offset in hours and minutes from the coordinated universal time (UTC)

- Current page number and total number of copies: The **page-number** and **num-pages** fields contain the current page number and the number of copies being printed of that page respectively. If the printer doesn't support multiple copies option, then the value of the **num-pages** field will always be "1".

- A billing information string (optional): The **job-billing** field contains a copy of the **job-billing** attribute provided with the IPP `create-job` or `print-job` requests. The value of this field is "-" if none of these requests were provided.

The following is an illustration of how the `page_log` might look and the actual items of the `page_log` file:

```
printer user job-id date-time page-number num-copies job-billing

cupsprinter kajol 302 [05/Jun/2008:15:23:46 +0100] 1 5 #it-dep

cupsprinter kajol 202 [05/Jun/2008:15:23:46 +0100] 2 5 #it-dep

cupsprinter kajol 302 [05/Jun/2008:15:23:46 +0100] 3 5 #it-dep

cupsprinter kajol 302 [05/Jun/2008:15:23:46 +0100] 4 5 #it-dep

cupsprinter1 hritik 303 [05/Jun/2008:15:25:22 +0100]
                                          1 200 #finance-dep
```

It denotes that the job ID `302`, printed on `cupsprinter` by user `kajol`, a 64-page job printed in three copies, billed to `#it-dep`. The next job with ID `303`, was set by user `hritik` and printed 200 copies of one–page, and is set to be billed to `#finance-dep`.

Flaws of the CUPS Quota system

As flexible as the CUPS quota system is, it has a few flaws that you will need to keep in mind:

- The CUPS quota system works only if the printers are working properly. If the printer hardware has failed, the log information may not be correct.

- CUPS counts the job pages that are being processed by the software (that is, going through the RIP) rather than the physical sheets successfully leaving the printing device. If there is a jam while say printing the tenth sheet out of 100, and the job is aborted by the printer, the page count will still show that 100 pages were processed for that job.

- With this system, there is no provision to set up quotas for individual users. Quotas can be turned on or off for individual users, but it is not possible to assign different quota levels. If you want to give senior management higher quotas than the rest of the employees, you cannot do this with CUPS.

- You cannot see how much of the quota users have left for the assigned time period nor how much they've used to date.

- When a user is not permitted to print due to quota restrictions, they do not receive a meaningful error message. CUPS merely displays **client-error-not-possible**, but does not tell them why.

Other Accounting Tools

Though CUPS has its own quota system, there are other accounting systems you can use with CUPS.

The most well-known and feature-rich free software package for print accounting and quotas is **PyKota** (`http://www.pykota.com/`). We will discuss this in detail in a moment.

A simple system based on reading out the hardware counter of network printers via SNMP is `accsnmp`. More information is available on:

`http://fritz.potsdam.edu/projects/cupsapps/`

There are other accounting tools that can be used with CUPS, including PrintAnalyzer, printbill, and LogReport.

You can find more information about PrintAanlyzer at:

`http://savannah.nongnu.org/projects/printanalyze/`

The information about printbill can be found at:

`http://ieee.uow.edu.au/~daniel/software/printbill/index.shtml`

You can also find out more information about LogReport at:

`http://www.logreport.org/`

PyKota

As we have seen, CUPS features its own simple print quota system which is not extensible and lacks many of the features which are present in PyKota. PyKota is a centralized and extensible print quota system for the Common UNIX Printing System.

PyKota inserts itself between the two CUPS functions where it basically snatches the job after CUPS rasters it, so that the various accounting operations can be performed. If the user is allowed to print then PyKota sends the print data to the appropriate CUPS backend.

PyKota is written entirely in Python and its software is distributed under the terms of the GNU General Public License Version 3 of the Free Software Foundation (`http://www.fsf.org/`).

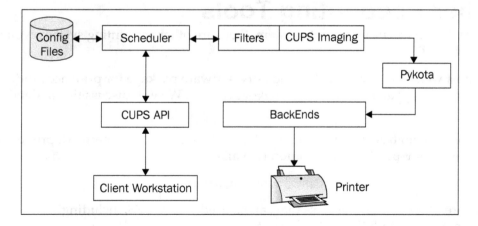

Features of PyKota:

The following are some of the important features of PyKota:

- It works with CUPS v 1.1.14 or higher. It is highly recommended that you use it with current releases.

- It can support any OS which can print through IPP, HTTP, LPR, or Samba services (such as GNU/Linux, Mac OSX, Windows 98 or higher).

- It works with database engines such as PostgreSQL, MySQL, SQLite, and OpenLDAP.

- It has universal support for almost all printers. This includes any physical or virtual printer that can report its internal page count through SNMP or PJL (Printer Job Language, which works over TCP/IP) as these protocols natively supports hardware accounting.

- It provides quota for individual printers, users, as well as groups.

- It supports sending automated email warnings to users and administrators.

- It has command line tools with very powerful options that allow you to manage quotas easily.

- It provides a web interface for the display of information about (but not administration of) quotas. It can display output in several different formats, including that of the `page_log` file.

- A single quota server can be used to provide centralized quotas for multiple printers and print servers.

- It has a configurable log system, which supports both `stderr` and `syslog`.

- Its offline documentation is included in SGML source form, DocBook DTD. You can compile it into other formats using the appropriate commands.

PyKota provides three different methods of implementation:

1. Hardware—In this method, Pykota queries the printer (via SNMP or Netatalk or any other method of your choice) for its internal pages count. The printer is queried both at the beginning and at the end of a print job, and then Pykota uses the difference in counters to reduce the user's account balance or increase the quota usage.

2. Software — This method counts the job's size in number of pages, and then this counter is delegated to any external command of your choice. Now the command should be able to read the job's data from its standard input and must output the job's size on its standard output. If any changes are made to the user account, they are reported immediately. Internally, it uses the code from `pkpgcounter` that can handle several Page Description Languages (PDLs).

A Page Description Language (PDL) is a computer language that describes the layout and contents of a printed page. The DSC compliant and binary PostScript, PCL3/4/5, PDF, PCLXL, ESC/P, DVI, TIFF, OpenDocument, Samsung QPDL, Samsung SPL, plain text, and so on are some examples of PDL.

To implement this method, you need to install `pkpgcounter` first. The `tar` files for `pkpgcounter` can be downloaded from Pykota website:

`http://www.pykota.com/software/pkpgcounter/download/tarballs`

You can get the install `pkpgcounter` in the following ways:

*   **subversion**: This method will provide the method to get and install the latest development release
*   **tar**: This method is used to install the latest stable release. It is the most popular method for UNIX and Linux platforms
*   **apt-get**: The Debian users can use this method which allows them to download and install the package using repository

You can find basic installation steps for the above mentioned methods here:

`http://www.pykota.com/software/pkpgcounter/download`

The following URL is the homepage of `pkpgcounter`, where you can find additional information:

`http://www.pykota.com/software/pkpgcounter`

3. Ink — This method uses the code of `pkpgcounter` to compute how much of each page is covered by ink in each color of a particular colorspace chosen between CMYK, CMY, RGB, and BW. The sum of these values is generated, which is then multiplied by a set of coefficients defined in PyKota's configuration files.

CMYK stands for cyan, magenta, yellow, and key (black) and is often referred to as process color or four color. It is a subtractive color model, used in color printing, also used to describe the printing process itself.

CMY stands for cyan, magenta, yellow, which are the subtractive primary colours, sometimes referred to as the secondary colors. There is no white in this system. The absence of all three will leave the white of the paper.

RGB stands for the three primary colors of light—Red, Green, and Blue. RGB can be described as the computer's native color space for capturing images and displaying them.

BW grayscale refers to the range of shades of grey for black and white (B&W) images. A normal BW image contains only two colors, black and white, and doesn't have any grey shade.

Checking Prerequisites and Downloading Application

The installation process is by far the most difficult part of using PyKota. You can get access to the official, stable release by purchasing a pass for a $25 or €25 from:

```
http://www.pykota.com/purchase
```

Eventhough PyKota is available under the terms of the GNU General Public License of the Free Software Foundation, version 3,the official packages repositories can be visited only after paying a nominal entry fee.

You can also obtain a megapack for a €7.99 fee from the PyKota web site:

```
http://www.pykota.com/buymegapack
```

The development release can be downloaded via web for free.

With PyKota, you need to install:

- Backends: LDAP, MySQL or PostgreSQL

- Dependencies: PyKota depends on other packages

The dependencies can be checked from the following URL:

```
http://www.pykota.com/wiki/Dependencies
```

The stable release provides an ISO file, which includes all of these dependencies along with the PyKota application.

Installation

It is recommended that you change to the directory where you want to extract the PyKota bundle:

`$cd /tmp/pykota`

It can be extracted using the following command:

`$tar -zxf pykota-m.nn_official.tar.gz`

To check whether any dependency is installed, change the directory path:

`$cd pykota-m.nn_official`

And execute the following python command that checks the missing dependency:

`$python checkdeps.py`

If dependencies are missing, then they should be installed first and then finally the PyKota installation should be done using the following command:

`$python setup.py install`

PyKota can only be configured using command line tools and not through a GUI. There are only a few commands with powerful options that can be used for managing quotas on printers, users, and groups. The following are some of the important commands that can be used with PyKota:

- `dumpykota`: The command extracts data from PyKota and outputs data in different formats such as comma separated values, semicolon separated values, tab separated values, and XML. The extracted data types can be of users, user groups, printers, membership of user groups or printer groups, quota entries of users or user groups, history of payments, print jobs, billing code and so on.

- `repykota`: This command generates reports by printer, user, and group. The output will be different for administrators and normal users. Administrator will see output for all the users and groups. If the command is executed by an end user, then he or she can only see the information about himself or herself and the group to which he or she belongs.

- `pkprinters`: This command is used to manage printers and printer groups.

- `pkusers`: Users and user groups can be managed by this command.

- `edpykota`: This command is used to create print quotas for users or groups on allowed printers.

- warnpykota: The command is useful in setting up warnings for end users when they exceed their print quota. If you want to send the notification in terms of warnings to end user at specific intervals, the command can be executed by setting it up as a cron job.

You can learn more about other these and other commands from the following URL:

```
http://www.pykota.com/wiki/CommandLineTools
```

Any additional information related to PyKota can be found from this URL:

```
http://www.pykota.com/software/pykota/
```

Summary

In this chapter, we have discussed quota management with CUPS. As a managed printer system, CUPS provides features to manage printers by setting up quotas. Currently there are a number of improvements such as more flexibility, advanced accounting, and support for other tools around quotas planned in the future versions of CUPS. Though CUPS has very limited internal features to handle complex scenarios, more can be achieved through a CUPS add-on quota system such as PyKota. It is a granular quota management system that has the ability to manage printers and users and can fill a gap left by CUPS built-in quota management system.

8
Monitoring CUPS

The Common UNIX Printing System (CUPS) is actually a printer management tool, and thus monitoring CUPS always remains a very essential activity to to make the best use of the resources available. Monitoring CUPS will allow us to take action quickly should something go wrong.

Using the lpstat Command

The `lpstat` command displays the status of the CUPS service, printers, classes, and jobs. It supports a number of options. If the command is used without any options, it displays the job queues for the current user:

```
$lpstat

cupstest-3 kajol 8192 Tue Aug 05 13:24:43 2008
cupstest-4 kajol 8192 Tue Aug 05 13:25:34 2008
```

To check whether the CUPS server is running, use the `-r` option.

```
$lpstat -r

scheduler is running

$lpstat -d

system default destination: cupsclass
```

The above command gives information about the default destination printer or class. The output following the command shows that the default destination of the system is cupsclass.

```
$lpstat -c cupsclass
```

This shows the printer class and the member printers belonging to that class. If a particular class is not specified, then the output shows all classes along with their member printers.

members of class cupsclass:

    cupsprinter1

    cupsprinter2

```
$lpstat -v cupsprinter2
```

The command above will show the device to which `cupsprinter1` is attached. If no printers are specified, then the output will list all printers along with `device-uri` information.

device for cupsprinter2: ipp://cupsserver.cupsgroup.org/printers/cupsprinter2

```
$lpstat -s
```

This shows a status summary for all printers and classes on the network. The summary includes the default destination, a list of classes and their member printers, and a list of printers and their associated devices. The output is equivalent to using the `-d`, `-c`, and `-v` options simultaneously.

system default destination: cupsclass

members of class cupsclass:

    cupsprinter1

    cupsprinter2

device for cupsprinter1: lpd://192.168.0.11/printers/cupsprinter1

device for cupsprinter2: ipp://cupsserver.cupsgroup.org/printers/cupsprinter2

```
$lpstat -a
```

This command shows if printers are currently accepting jobs. If no printers are specified, then it will list all printers.

cupsprinter1 accepting requests since Mon 16 Jun 2008 02:28:14 PM IST

cupsprinter2 accepting requests since Wed 18 Jun 2008 11:07:23 AM IST

```
$lpstat -p cupsprinter1
```

This shows whether the printer `cupsprinter1` is enabled and if it is currently printing a job. If no printers are specified then all the printers are listed.

printer cupsprinter1 is idle. enabled since Mon 16 Jun 2008 02:28:14 PM IST

```
$lpstat -o
```

This shows the job queues on the specified destinations. If no destinations are specified then all jobs are shown.

`$lpstat -t`

This displays status information for all printers, which is equivalent to using the `-r`, `-d`, `-c`, `-v`, `-a`, `-p`, and `-o` options.

scheduler is running

system default destination: cupsclass

members of class cupsclass:

> **cupsprinter1**

> **cupsprinter2**

device for cupsprinter1: lpd://192.168.0.11/printers/cupsprinter1

device for cupsprinter2: ipp://cupsserver.cupsgroup.org/printers/cupsprinter2

cupsprinter1 accepting requests since Mon 16 Jun 2008 02:28:14 PM IST

cupsprinter2 accepting requests since Wed 18 Jun 2008 11:07:23 AM IST

printer cupsprinter1 is idle. enabled since Mon 16 Jun 2008 02:28:14 PM IST

printer cupsprinter2 now printing cupsprinter2-5711. enabled since Wed 18 Jun 2008 03:12:55 PM IST

> **Printer is now on-line.**

cupsprinter2-5711   kajol   1449984 Wed 18 Jun 2008 03:12:55 PM IST

`$lpstat -l`

This command displays printers, classes, or jobs in a long list.

`$lpstat -u`

This shows a list of print jobs queued by the specified users. If no users are specified, it lists the jobs queued by the current user.

cupsprinter2-5711   kajol   1449984 Wed 18 Jun 2008 03:12:55 PM IST

`$lpstat -h 192.168.0.11:631`

The above command specifies an alternative server for CUPS. It uses the port number that is specified along with the server. If no port is specified, then it will connect to the default port 631.

```
$lpstat -U username
```

You can specify an alternative username with the -U option.

```
$lpstat -R : $lpstat -W all
```

This shows the ranking of print jobs.

This command specifies which jobs to show, complete, incomplete (the default), or all. This option must appear before the -o option and any printer names:

```
$lpstat -W completed -o cupsprinter2
```

The output will be as follows

cupsprinter2-5709	kajol	483328	Wed 18 Jun 2008 03:10:45 PM IST
cupsprinter2-5710	kajol	97280	Wed 18 Jun 2008 03:12:18 PM IST
cupsprinter2-5711	kajol	1449984	Wed 18 Jun 2008 03:12:55 PM IST
cupsprinter2-5712	kajol	8192	Wed 18 Jun 2008 03:22:31 PM IST
cupsprinter2-5713	kajol	9216	Wed 18 Jun 2008 03:23:38 PM IST
cupsprinter2-5714	kajol	9216	Wed 18 Jun 2008 03:24:23 PM IST

```
$lpstat -E
```

This command forces encryption when connecting to a print server.

Overview of the access_log File

The access_log file lists each HTTP resource that is accessed by a web browser or a CUPS/IPP client. The file contains the lines specified in the following log format, which is an extension of the Common Log Format used by many web servers and web reporting tools.

> The "Common Log Format" is a standardized text file format used by web servers while generating log files. As the format is standardized, the files may be analyzed by a variety of analysis programs.

The syntax of the access_log file is :

```
host group user date-time \"method resource version\"
    status bytes iPP-operations ipp-status
```

- Hostname: The host field contains the IP address or hostname that can be seen if the "HostNameLookups" directive is enabled in the cupsd.conf file.

- Groupname: The value always remains "-" for the group field.

- Username: The user field is the authenticated username of the requesting user. If no authenticated username is supplied for the request, then this field contains "-".

- Time of printing: The date-time field refers to the date and time of the request in local time. Here, the "local time" denotes the time of the print server. The syntax is quite similar to that of the page_log file, which we have already discussed in Chapter 7.

- Method: The method field is the HTTP method used (GET,OPTIONS,PUT,POST, and so forth).

    ° GET: These requests are used to get files from the server, both for the web interface and for the configuration and log files.

    ° OPTIONS: These requests are used to upgrade connections to TLS encryption.

    ° PUT: These requests are used to upload the configuration files.

    ° POST: These requests are used for web interface forms and IPP requests.

- Resource: The resource field records the filename of the requested resource.

- Version: The version field is the HTTP specification version used by the client. The value is always "HTTP/1.1" for CUPS clients.

- Status: The status gives the HTTP result status of the request. Usually, the status code is 200, which suggests an **OK** status. If the code is 401, then it suggests **Unauthorized Access**. The following are some of the Status Codes along with their meaning:

    ° 200: This status code denotes successful operation, which means **OK** status.

    ° 201: This denotes that a file has been created or modified successfully.

    ° 304: The code 304 suggests that the requested file has not changed.

    ° 400: This means **Bad HTTP request**, as in some malicious program is trying to access your server.

- ○ 401: The code 401 means there has been an attempt at **Unauthorized Access**. The correct login information (username + password) is required to authenticate.

- ○ 403: This code refers to **Access is forbidden**, which means that a client tried to access a resource or file for which they did not have permission.

- ○ 404: The code 404 denotes that the requested file or resource **does not exist**.

- ○ 405: This code means the **URL access method is not allowed**. It means a web browser is using the server as a proxy.

- ○ 413: This means that the request is too large. It occurs when the client tries to print a file larger than the `MaxRequestSize` allows.

- ○ 426: A server may indicate that a client request cannot be completed without TLS using the **Upgrade Required** status code, which must include an upgrade header field specifying the token of the required TLS version

- ○ 500: This code denotes that there is a **server error**. The log for the error can be checked in the server's `error_log` file. We will discuss the `error_log` file briefly later in this chapter.

- ○ 501: The client has requested encryption, but the **encryption support is not enabled** on the server.

- ○ 505: The given **HTTP version number is not supported**, which normally happens when some malicious program is trying to access your server.

- ○ You can get more information about these status codes at:

  `http://www.w3.org/Protocols/rfc2616/rfc2616-sec10.html`

- • `Size in bytes`: The `bytes` field contains the number of bytes in the request. For POST requests, the bytes field contains the number of bytes that were received from the client.

- • `IPP Operations`: The `ipp-operation` field denotes the the name of the CUPS-IPP operation that performed the POST request. The value for the description of CUPS-IPP operation is given here:

Operation Name	Description
Print-Job	Print a file
Validate-Job	Validate job attributes
Create-Job	Create a print job
Send-Document	Send a file for a print job
Cancel-Job	Cancel a print job
Get-Job-Attributes	Get job attributes
Get-Jobs	Get all jobs
Get-Printer-Attributes	Get printer attributes
Hold-Job	Hold a job for printing
Release-Job	Release a job for printing
Restart-Job	Restart a print job
Pause-Printer	Pause printing on a printer
Resume-Printer	Resume printing on a printer
Purge-Jobs	Purge all jobs
Set-Job-Attributes	Set attributes for a pending or held job
Create-Printer-Subscription	Create a subscription associated with a printer or the server
Create-Job-Subscription	Create a subscription associated with a job
Get-Subscription-Attributes	Get the attributes for a subscription
Get-Subscriptions	Get the attributes for zero or more subscriptions
Renew-Subscription	Renew a subscription
Cancel-Subscription	Cancel a subscription
Get-Notifications	Get notification events for `ippget` subscriptions
Enable-Printer	Accept jobs on a printer
Disable-Printer	Reject jobs on a printer
CUPS-Get-Default	Get the default destination
CUPS-Get-Printers	Get all of the available printers
CUPS-Add-Modify-Printer	Add or modify a printer
CUPS-Delete-Printer	Delete a printer
CUPS-Get-Classes	Get all of the available printer classes
CUPS-Add-Modify-Class	Add or modify a printer class
CUPS-Delete-Class	Delete a printer class
CUPS-Accept-Jobs	Accept jobs on a printer or printer class
CUPS-Reject-Jobs	Reject jobs on a printer or printer class
CUPS-Set-Default	Set the default destination

Operation Name	Description
CUPS-Get-Devices	Get all the available devices
CUPS-Get-PPDs	Get all the available PPDs
CUPS-Move-Job	Move a job to a different printer
CUPS-Authenticate-Job	Authenticate a job for printing
CUPS-Get-PPD	Get a PPD file

- IPP status: The `ipp-status` field denotes the IPP-status code name for the POST requests. The value for this field will be "-" for non-IPP requests. With each IPP operation, a number of IPP statuses are possible. The default information can be found at the following URL:

  `http://www.cups.org/documentation.php/spec-ipp.html`

  Here are the example lines from an `access_log` file:

```
192.168.0.35 - - [18/Jun/2008:10:46:37 +0530]
                           "GET /admin HTTP/1.1" 401 0 - -

192.168.0.33 - - [18/Jun/2008:10:38:30 +0530]
                   "POST /printers/cupsprinter1HTTP/1.1"
            200 130 Get-Printer-Attributes successful-ok

localhost - - [18/Jun/2008:10:36:38 +0530] "POST / HTTP/1.1"
                   200 182 CUPS-Get-Printers successful-ok

192.168.5.19 - - [05/Jun/2008:17:46:04 +0530]
                   "POST /printers/ HTTP/1.1" 200 159656
      Print-Job client-error-document-format-not-supported
```

Overview of the error_log File

The `error_log` file displays messages from the scheduler such as "warnings", "errors", and so on:

- Level: The `level` field contains the type of message:

  A: Alert message (LogLevel alert)

  C: Critical error message (LogLevel crit)

  D: Debugging message (LogLevel debug)

  d: Detailed debugging message (LogLevel debug2)

E: Normal error message (LogLevel error)

I: Informational message (LogLevel info)

N: Notice message (LogLevel notice)

W: Warning message (LogLevel warn)

X: Emergency error message (LogLevel emerg)

- Time of Printing: The `date-time` field contains the date and time when the page started printing. The format of this field is identical to the `data-time` field in the **page_log** file.

- Message: This field contains free-form textual messages. In the following examples of the `error_log` files, the last field contains messages of this type.

The syntax for the `error_log` file is `level date-time message`.

The following are the some examples of entries in the `error_log` file :

```
I [05/Jun/2008:15:23:46 +0530] Job 224 queued on 'cupsprinter' by
'hritik'.
I [05/Jun/2008:15:23:46 +0530] Job 304 was cancelled by 'aamir'.
D [18/Jun/2008:14:53:18 +0530] cupsdProcessIPPRequest: 12 status_
code=0 (successful-ok)
I [05/Jun/2008:15:23:46 +0530] Job 309 queued on 'cupsprnter' by
'kajol'.
I [05/Jun/2008:15:23:46 +0530] Job 322 queued on 'cupsprinter' by
'kajol'.
```

How SNMP Helps Search for Network Printers

As we have discussed in earlier chapters, most of the network printers that CUPS uses use one of these three TCP/IP-based protocols:

- AppSocket
- Internet Printing Protocol (IPP)
- Line Printer Daemon (LPD)

Now apart from these protocols, CUPS also uses another networking protocol —
SNMP that is used to search for networked printers. In future, CUPS will support
other networking protocols such as multicast DNS service for the same purpose.
First, we will discuss how the configuration of SNMP is done within CUPS (`/etc/`
`cups/snmp.conf`), and then we will check how it actually works in the web interface.
Before we start discussing the `snmp.conf` file, let us see the some of the key terms
related to the file.

The SNMP stands for "Simple Network Management Protocol" and consists of three
key components:

- Managed Devices: A managed device is a node that has an SNMP agent,
  and resides on a managed network. These devices can be routers and access
  servers, switches, bridges, hubs, computer hosts, or printers.

- Agents: An agent is a software module residing within a device. This agent
  translates information into a format compatible with SNMP.

- Network-Management Systems (NMS): An NMS runs monitoring
  applications, which provide the bulk of processing and memory resources
  required for network management.

Overview of snmp.conf

Since CUPS is a printer management system working on networking protocols,
SNMP will be an integral part of the CUPS system. The configuration file `snmp.conf`
resides in `/etc/cups`, and contains various directives, which determine the behavior
of the SNMP printer discovery backend. The file contains the directive name
followed by its value. The number sign "#" is used to specify the comments.

Currently, the SNMPv1 protocol is being used by the SNMP backend to discover
network printers in CUPS and help to determine the correct device URI and the
vendor, and the driver of each printer. IT expects that the future release of CUPS will
have support for all SNMP versions including, SNMPv2, v2c, and v3.

SNMP actually collects information from the MIB (Management Information Base)
host along with port probes to get this information. It is expected that, in future,
CUPS will start supporting the new Port monitor MIB as well. The following are
some of the key definitions related to MIB.

MIB stands for Management Information Base, which is a collection of information organized hierarchically. It is accessed using a protocol such as SNMP. There are two types of MIBs:

- Scalar: Scalar objects define a single object instance.
- Tabular: Tabular objects define multiple related object instances grouped in MIB tables.

Address

This directive specifies a broadcast address to be used when discovering printers. We can also specify multiple address lines to scan different subnets.

The following examples show various values that can be given along with this directive. The value @LOCAL denotes broadcasting across all LANs. The value @LOCAL is also the default value for this directive, while @IF broadcasts to the named interface. You can also provide the broadcast address or the IP address with the directive for which broadcasting needs to be done.

```
Address @LOCAL
Address @IF(name)
Address 255.255.255.255
Address 192.168.0.255
```

Community

The directive Community is used to specify a community name that can be used while discovering printers. The default value for this directive is public. You can specify multiple lines to scan different SNMP communities.

```
Community public
Community cupsgrp
Community packtpub
```

DebugLevel

The DebugLevel directive denotes the specified debugging level to be used when searching for network printers. This directive can have four debugging levels. It starts from 0 and ends with 3:

```
DebugLevel 0
DebugLevel 1
DebugLevel 2
DebugLevel 3
```

In the above example:

Level 0: It is used to disable debugging, and hence does not produce any debugging information. It is also the default level of debugging.

Level 1: It generates basic debugging information. We will explain this later in the chapter.

Level 2: It also prints the SNMP messages along with the basic debugging information.

Level 3: This level adds a hexadecimal code dump of the network data.

DeviceURI

The directive `DeviceURI` is used to specify a regular expression, which is enclosed in double quotes. This URI is checked with the SNMP device description OID returned by a printer.

 OID stands for Object Identifier. These uniquely identify the objects managed in the MIB hierarchy. This hierarchy can be depicted as a tree, the levels of which are assigned by different organizations.

If the given description matches the regular expression, the CUPS backend will list each of the device URIs that follow by regular expression.

The following are some examples that show `DeviceURI` directives along with the regular expression and the actual device URI.

Please note that here any occurrence of `%s` is replaced by the device's IP address or hostname. Here `xx`, `yyy`, and `zzzz` are a part of the regular expressions. We can use the make and model of the printer for these.

If no URIs are listed within this directive, then the requested device will be ignored. These directives are processed serially in the order specified in the `snmp.conf` file, until a match is found. The following are some of the examples of the directive:

```
DeviceURI "xx.*" socket://%s
DeviceURI "*LaseJet.*" socket://%s:9100 socket://%s:9101
DeviceURI "yyy.*"
DeviceURI "zzzz.*Desk.*" lpd://%s/printer
```

HostNameLookups

This directive is used to specify whether the printer addresses are converted to hostnames, or remain as numeric IP addresses. The default value for this directive is `off`.

```
HostNameLookups off
HostNameLookups on
```

MaxRunTime

The `MaxRunTime` directive specifies the maximum time (in seconds) spent by the SNMP backend searching for printers across the network. As the following example shows, it can contain any integer value. The default value for this directive is 10 seconds.

```
MaxRunTime 10
MaxRunTime 480
```

How SNMP Behaves in the CUPS Web Interface

In the CUPS web interface under the **Administration** tab, the option **Find New Printers** is used to discover printers that support SNMPv1.

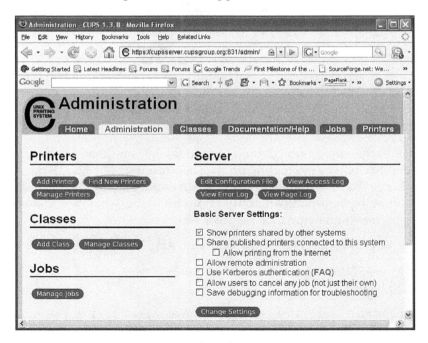

This will search and list the available network printers. The discovery of printers is based on the directive configuration done in the /etc/cups/snmp.conf file. On the basis of the search list, you can add a printer using the **Add This Printer** option. The process is very similar to the **Add Printer** wizard, which we have already discussed in Chapter 3.

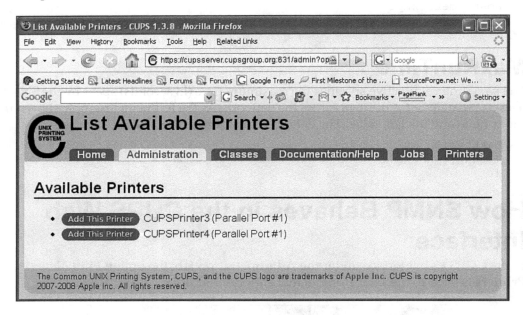

Overview of Basic Debugging in CUPS-SNMP

In the snmp.conf, we started discussion about various debugging levels in CUPS support. If the directive DebugLevel is set to anything other than 0, you will get the output accordingly. The debugging mode can be made active using the following command.

As the SNMP backend supports debugging mode, the command for setting up debugging mode changes depending on the shell prompt. The SNMP backend is located at /usr/lib/cups/backend/snmp when using the Bourne, Bash, Z, or Korn shells. The following command will output verbose debugging information into the cupssnmp.log file when using those shells:

```
$CUPS_DEBUG_LEVEL=1 /usr/lib/cups/backend/snmp 2>&1 | tee cupssnmp.log
```

On Mac OS X, the SNMP backend is located /usr/libexec/cups. The following command will be used:

```
$CUPS_DEBUG_LEVEL=1 /usr/libexec/cups/backend/snmp 2>&1 | tee cupssnmp.log
```

If you are using the C or Tcsh shells, you can use the following command:

```
$(setenv CUPS_DEBUG_LEVEL 1; /usr/lib/cups/backend/snmp) |& tee
cupssnmp.log
```

An example of the output might look like this:

DEBUG: Scanning for devices in "public" via "@LOCAL"...

DEBUG: 0.000 Sending 46 bytes to 192.168.0.255...

DEBUG: 0.001 Received 50 bytes from 192.168.0.250...

DEBUG: community="public"

DEBUG: request-id=1213875587

DEBUG: error-status=0

DEBUG: 1.001 Scan complete!

The above output shows that doesn't find any printer at the specified DeviceURI. The above shows the output at the basic debugging level; more information can be found if we use level 2 or 3.

Overview of mailto.conf

The CUPS provides the facility to send notifications through email. It can be done by integrating the local mail server with CUPS. The configuration file is /etc/cups/mailto.conf, and contains several directives and the characteristics and behavior of the local mail server and email notification for CUPS. We normally use each of the following directives in our daily communication done through mail.

The Cc Directive

The directive Cc (carbon copy) is used to specify an additional recipient for all email notifications. By default, the value directive is not set and the email is sent only to the administrator. The following examples shows that how email IDs can be specified with this directive.

```
Cc kajol@cupsgrp.com
Cc Kajol Shah <ks@cupsgrp.com>
```

The From Directive

This directive is used to specify the sender's name in the email notifications. By default, the `ServerAdmin` address specified in the `cupsd.conf` file is used. The following are some examples that show how the sender's email is specified with this directive:

```
From cupsadmin@cupsgrp.com
From Your CUPS Printer <cupsadmin@cupsgrp.com>
```

The Sendmail Directive

The directive `Sendmail` specifies the command to run and deliver an email locally. If there is an `SMTPServer` directive, then this directive cannot be used. If both directives appear in the `mailto.conf` file, then only the last directive is used. The following example shows how this directive can be specified. The default value for this directive is `/usr/sbin/sendmail`.

```
Sendmail /usr/sbin/sendmail
Sendmail /usr/lib/sendmail -bm -i
```

The SMTPServer Directive

This directive is used to specify an IP address or hostname of an SMTP mail server. As we have seen previously, this directive cannot be used with the `Sendmail` directive, and if both `Sendmail` and `SMTPServer` directives don't appear in the `mailto.conf` file, then the default `Sendmail` will be considered. The following are examples of the SMTP server:

```
SMTPServer mail.mailforcups.com
SMTPServer 192.168.0.17
```

The Subject Directive

The `Subject` directive is used if you want to prefix some text to the subject line in each email that CUPS sends out. The following examples show how a prefix can be specified with this directive. By default, no prefix string is added:

```
Subject [CUPS_ALERTS]
Subject URGENT CUPS NOTICE
```

Monitoring SNMP Printers

As discussed, CUPS supports SNMPv1 for discovering SNMP enabled printers. This Simple Network Management Protocol-SNMP is used for managing networking printers. We can use any network monitoring tools that supports SNMP for monitoring these SNMP-enabled printers. You can check various open-source network monitoring tools at:

`http://www.openxtra.co.uk/network-management/monitor/open-source/`

I would recommend you to use Cacti, which is a frontend to an RRDTool (Round Robin Database Tool) that collects and stores data in a MySQL database. The frontend is completely written in PHP. The advantage of Cacti over other network monitoring tool is that it has built-in SNMP capabilities and like other monitoring tools such as Nagios, it has its internal mechanism to check certain aspects of the infrastructure. It also provides a frontend for maintaining customized scripts, which an administrator normally creates. But the most important factor is that it is much easier to configure than Nagios.

RRDTool is a system that stores high performance logging data and displays related time-series graphs. You can get more information about RRDTool from:

`http://oss.oetiker.ch/rrdtool/`

Downloading and Installing Cacti

The pre-requisites of Cacti include MySQL database, PHP, RRDTool, net-snmp, and PHP supported web servers such as Apache or IIS. You can get detailed information about the pre-requisites for Cacti installation at:

`http://www.cacti.net/downloads/docs/html/requirements.html`

The current stable release of Cacti is 0.8.7b. You can download various versions of Cacti for different platforms from:

`http://www.cacti.net/download_cacti.php`

You can get installation information for Cacti and its pre-requisites on the UNIX/Linux platform from:

`http://www.cacti.net/downloads/docs/html/install_unix.html`

The following URL will help you install Cacti on the Windows platform:

`http://www.cacti.net/downloads/docs/html/install_windows.html`

Gentoo, Debian, Fedora, and Suse Linux users can use update managers for installing Cacti. The advantages of using these features are that they take care of the software's pre-requisites before the software installation. You can get commands for installing/upgrading Cacti for these platforms at:

`http://www.cacti.net/download_cacti.php`

Once all the prerequisites and configuration of Cacti are done as per the details mentioned at the above URL, you can start installing Cacti by starting your web browser, which shows the guide for the installation instructions and license information.

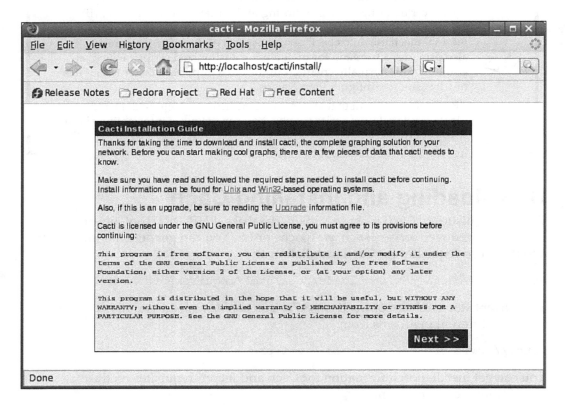

You can proceed further by clicking on **Next**. The next screen shows two options for a new install or an upgrade. If you want to do fresh installation, use the option **New Install** and click on **Next**. The screen also displays some useful information such as database user, database hostname, database name, and OS that was specified while configuring Cacti.

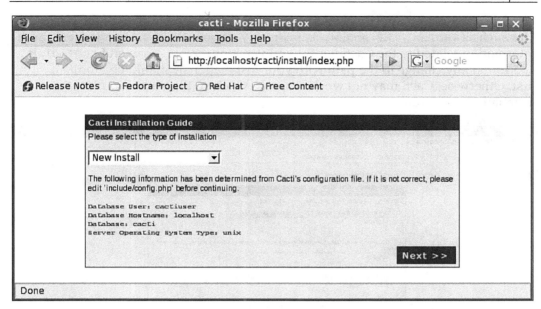

If you want to upgrade the Cacti, follow the instructions mentioned here:

`http://www.cacti.net/downloads/docs/html/upgrade.html`

And then select the **upgrade from cacti-current-version** option and click on **Next** to proceed further.

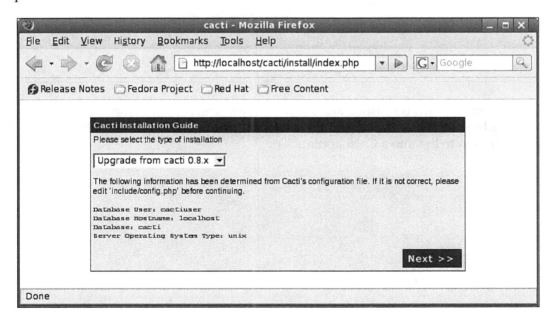

The following screen appears, which shows the recommended path of the binary files such as RRDTool, PHP, snmpwalk, snmpgetV, snmpbulkwalk, snmpgetnext, and information related to the Cacti log file and versions for net-snmp and RRDTool. If you found any change in the path with your installation, it should be modified first. Otherwise, Cacti may not work properly. Click on **Finish** to complete the installation procedure.

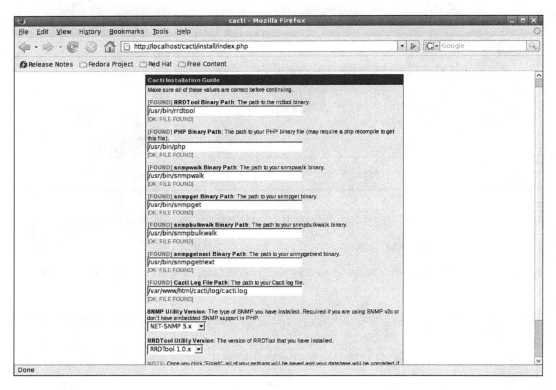

Once the installation is finished and the next screen will ask for authentication. You need to use the username and the password mentioned in your database configuration to log into a Cacti application:

You can use default login information to log in for the first time. Once you click on **Login**, the next screen will force you to change your password.

Once the password is changed, you can see the main page of Cacti that contains two major tabs: console and graphs apart from other generalized options. The **console** tab contains various options related to the template and graphs management, whereas the **graphs** tab contains related graphs.

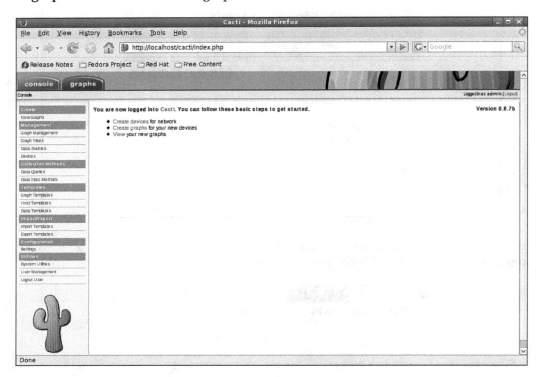

Features of Cacti

Cacti supports various features such as graphs, graph display, data source, data gathering, scripts, templates, and user management. You can find more information on this at:

`http://cacti.net/features.php`

You can get information about the various additional scripts:

`http://cacti.net/additional_scripts.php`

Configuring an SNMP Printer with Cacti

In this section, we are going to integrate an SNMP Printer as a network device in Cacti. Before we start discussing, let's first understand how Cacti works. Like any other network monitoring functionality Cacti also depends on three factors:

- Data Retrieval
- Data Storage
- Data Presentation

You can get detailed information on this at:

`http://www.cacti.net/downloads/docs/html/operating_principles.html`

The greatest strength of Cacti is its graphing. To make the graphs of a networking device available, the device should be configured in Cacti. You can configure it by clicking on **Device** and then on **Add** by selecting the proper options. The following screen will appear which shows general information on the device and the protocol you want to use for polling. The first two fields of **Description** and **Hostname** are important as they identify the device you are creating. If you are not sure about how to use other options in the **Host Template** field, it is recommended that you use **Generic SNMP-enabled Host**. You can keep the remaining fields as the default if you are sure of an option. The screen is divided in two parts for better display.

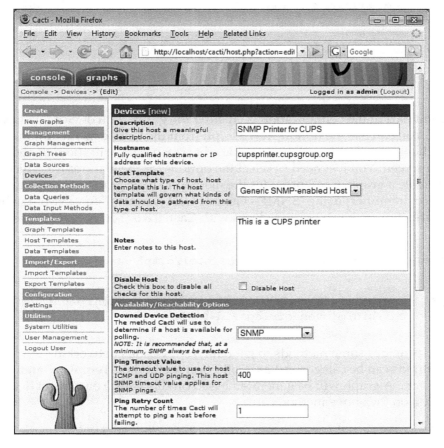

The second part contains options for SNMP such as versions, ports, and so on. Select the version of SNMP and the other options properly and then click on **Create** to make the device available for use.

You can get detailed information about the device options at:
`http://www.cacti.net/downloads/docs/html/graph_howto.html`

SNMP Options	
SNMP Version Choose the SNMP version for this device.	Version 1 ▾
SNMP Community SNMP read community for this device.	public
SNMP Port Enter the UDP port number to use for SNMP (default is 161).	161
SNMP Timeout The maximum number of milliseconds Cacti will wait for an SNMP response (does not work with php-snmp support).	500
Maximum OID's Per Get Request Specified the number of OID's that can be obtained in a single SNMP Get request. *NOTE: This feature only works when using Spine*	10
	cancel · create

The second part of the configuration is creating the graph for a device you have specified. You can use the option **New Graph** from the **Create** menu option, or you can choose the **Create** option from the edit screen. This will show on the following screen. You just need to select the options for the features for which you want to create a graph. Cacti provides the method to have graph value for a single OID (Object Identifier) using "SNMP - Generic OID Template" for SNMP-enabled services.This feature has been introduces with Cacti 0.8.5. You will get to see more on this at:

`http://www.cacti.net/downloads/docs/html/graph_snmp_oid.html`

 You can get a list of all SNMP OIDs at `http://www.mibdepot.com/cgi-bin/mibvendors.cgi?id=91732`.

Cacti also provides some methods to get data from various networking devices. These methods can be categorized as "Collection Methods", "Template" and "PHP Script Server". A graph will be generated based on this data. You can get detailed information on the above methods at:

`http://www.cacti.net/downloads/docs/html/advanced_topics.html`

The Collection Methods are again divided into the following two methods:

- Data Input Methods
- Data Queries

We will be discussing the "Data Queries" as we have shown one of the methods in our following example. This "Data Query" method again provides two ways for querying: SNMP query and Script query. The only difference between these two query methods is the way they obtain data.

These data queries contain two parts: a definition for Cacti and an XML file.

The XML file gives the required information and the method for its retrieval, whereas the definition part informs Cacti where to find this XML file and related data queries with proper graph templates. You can get detailed information on this at:

`http://www.cacti.net/downloads/docs/html/data_queries.html`

Here, we will be discussing the SNMP query for which I have created an XML file. You can use the **Data Queries** navigation link in the **Collection Methods** menu. You will have to supply a **Name**, and a **Description**. The other two fields of data input are important, which show the XML path of your data query and the method.

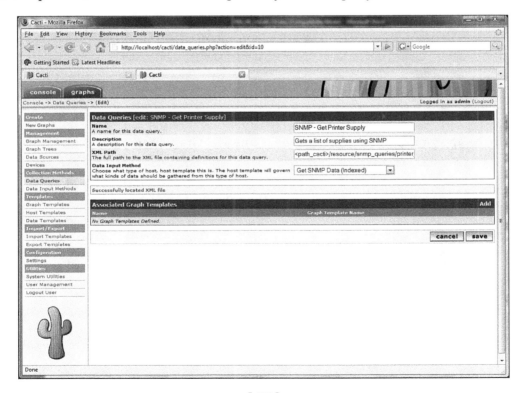

To generate a graph using a template for this data query, click on **Add** as highlighted in the previous screenshot. You will get a new screen as follows:

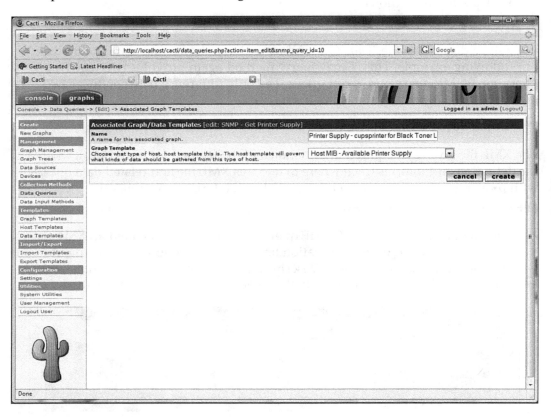

Fill in the appropriate information in the **Name** and **Graph Template** fields.

 You can import a new Graph/Host/Data template using the **Import Template** option from the **Import/Export** menu.

This should generate an appropriate graph for you.

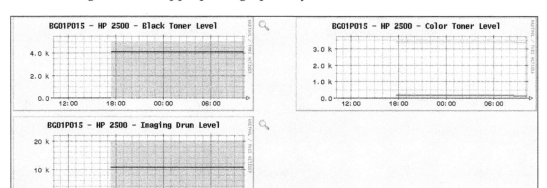

The above graph shows the toner level for color and black and white printers, and the drum level for `cupsprinter`.

Summary

In this chapter, we have discussed how to monitor printers and print jobs using CUPS. You've seen how to use the `lpstat` command, the `access_log` file and the `error_log` file to help you monitor printing on your network. We have also discussed how SNMP helps CUPS to search for printers. We have seen how the setup of email helps users, and then the administrator, in conveying some important messages. Finally, we also discussed how Cacti can be used to monitor our printer with the help of SNMP.

9
File Typing and Filtering

Since CUPS is a modular software, it is able to manage thousands of printer models. CUPS also utilizes the printers' drivers/filters and PPDs from different sources. It is very easy for any third-party software developers or hardware vendors of printers to incorporate their own drivers or filters within the CUPS framework. Foomatic, the Gimp-Print project and TurboPrint shareware that we discussed in the *Printer Driver* section of Chapter 3, are examples that conclude this. The CUPS internal framework also consists of various filters that are flexible enough to produce the desired result.

Architecture—CUPS Filtering System

The CUPS filtering system is distributed into three different layers:

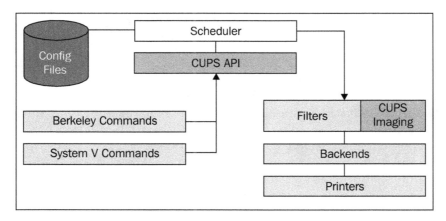

If we look at UNIX and Linux printing systems, individual applications are responsible for creating the printing output rather than the X window system or the OS kernel, which are independent of any application's behavior. Most applications use PostScript, but PostScript offers many ways to handle print output. We will discuss those methods here:

- **Converter:** Pages cannot be directly printed in formats such as PDF, GIF, and so on. Hence they generally require a conversion to PostScript, which is the only format CUPS can understand.

- **Filter:** Once the pages are converted into the PostScript file format, it will then be sent to the printer filter. This filter is nothing but a built-in interpreter called a "Raster Image Processor" (RIP). The RIP converts PostScript file into high-resolution raster images for printing as we can see here in the following figure. It shows a printing mechanism to a PostScript printer. The real PostScript printers such as Adobe, HP LaserJet that have the postscript engine in them and the GS generic filter are examples of printer filters that can understand PostScript.

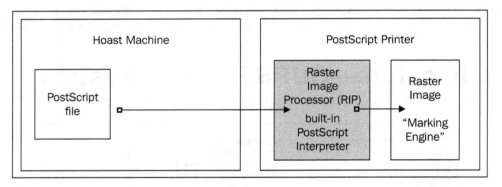

If the printer layer doesn't understand PostScript, then the PostScript will be sent to an external RIP that will eventually convert PostScript file into raster image, the format that is easily understood by the non-PostScript printer filters. The Ghostscript is the most popular and effective Raster Image Processor for non-PostScript Printers. Non-PostScript printer filters are used for printers that use PCL emulation or those that use different, proprietary protocols.

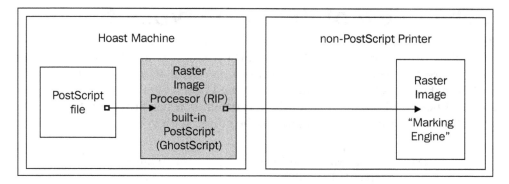

Ghostscript is the integral part of CUPS filtering architecture. The process of rasterizing a PostScript file into a native bit map image is done in two stages:

- In the first stage, a Ghostscript device called "cups" is used that produces a generic raster format called the "CUPS raster".

- In the second stage a "raster driver" is used that converts the generic CUPS raster to a device-specific raster. You can check whether the installed Ghostscript version has the "cups" device compiled using the following command:

```
$gs -h | grep cups
```

To have "cups" as a device in Ghostscript, you either need to patch GNU Ghostscript and recompile it, or use the ESP GhostScript. ESP Ghostscript will be a better choice as it supports not just CUPS, but over 300 other devices. Comparatively, GNU Ghostscript doesn't have much device support.

The "Foomatic/cupsomatic" software from openprinting.org uses the classical Ghostscript approach, which uses devices other than "cups". However, the best result can be achieved by ESP Ghostscript as it supports the newer software, "Foomatic-rip".

- **Backend:** The printer filters convert PostScript or raster data file into "raw" data format. This format is then sent to printer with the help of the backend.

If we want to enable raw printing support in CUPS, the information needs to be passed to CUPS. This can be done by configuring the required information in two files `mime.types` and `mime.convs` that are present in the `/etc/cups` directory. These files define the standard file types and filters that are available on the system. Let us discuss both these files in detail.

An Overview of the mime.types file

CUPS provides a MIME-based file typing and filtering mechanism to convert files to a printable format for each printer. On start up, CUPS reads the MIME database files in the directory /etc/cups with a suffix *.types. It also includes the mime. types file that defines the information about the known file types. These files consist of rules that help CUPS recognize a MIME type when it performs autotyping. These database files are plain ASCII text, and can be edited with your favorite text editor.

MIME types describe a file format in a non-ambiguous way. MIME types are separated into different categories such as main_category or minor_category, and they are registered with IANA (Internet Assigning Numbers Authority). Vendors may register their own proprietary file formats with IANA, provided they explain the method to recognize the format in a unique and unambiguous method.

Each line of the file starts with the MIME type and may be followed by one or more file type recognition rules. Its syntax looks like this:

```
super/type rule[rule1.....ruleN]
text/xml        xml xsl \
printable(0,1024) + \
(string(0,"<XML>") string(0,"<!DOCTYPE"))
application/x-javascript    js string(0,%JS)
application/postscript  ai eps ps string(0,%!) string(0,<04>%!)
```

- The first two rules indicate that any file with an extension of .xml or .xsl is an XML file. These two rules deal solely with the name of the file being typed. This is useful when the original filename is known. However, the server doesn't have a filename while working with print files.

- The third rule says that any file whose first 1024 characters are printable text, and starts with the strings <XML> or <!DOCTYPE> is also an XML file. However, this rule automatically figures out the file type based upon the contents of the file instead.

- The forth rule says that if a filename begins with the suffix .js or with the string %JS, then it is a PDF file.

- The fifth rule indicates that if the filename has one of these suffixes — .ai, .eps, .ps, or if the file starts with one of these strings — %! or <04>%!, it is a generic PostScript file.

The other available tests that should be applied as per the previously mentioned syntax are:

- `+` — Logical AND
- `,` or whitespace — Logical OR
- `!` — Negated or Logical NOT
- `( expr )` — Parenthesis for expression grouping
- `match("pattern")` — It matches the pattern on the filename
- `ascii(offset,length)` — True if bytes are valid and printable ASCII (CR, NL, TAB, BS, 32-126)
- `printable(offset,length)` — True if bytes are printable 8-bit chars (CR, NL, TAB, BS, 32-126, 128-254)
- `string(offset,"string")` — True if bytes are identical to string
- `istring(offset,"string")` — True if case-insensitive comparison of bytes is identical
- `char(offset,value)` — True if bytes are identical
- `short(offset,value)` — True if 16-bit integer is identical (network or big-endian byte order)
- `int(offset,value)` — True if 32-bit integer is identical (network or big-endian byte order)
- `locale("string")` — True if the current locale matches the string
- `extension` — Pattern match on `*.extension`
- `contains(offset,range,"string")` — True if the range of bytes contains the string

All numeric values can be decimal (456), octal (0456), or hexadecimal (0x456) as desired.

The strings can be in quotes, all by themselves, as a string of hexadecimal values, or some combination thereof:

```
"cupsstring"
'cupsstring'
cupsstr
<727372696e67>
<7273>ring
```

The rules can continue on multiple lines using the backslash (\) character. A more complex example is the image/jpeg rule:

```
image/jpeg        jpeg jpg jpe string(0,<FEE7FF>) &&\
(char(3,0xf0) char(3,0xf1) char(3,0xf2) char(3,0xf3)\
char(3,0xf4) char(3,0xf5) char(3,0xf6) char(3,0xf7)\
char(3,0xf8) char(3,0xf9) char(3,0xfa) char(3,0xfb)\
char(3,0xfc) char(3,0xfd) char(3,0xfe) char(3,0xff))
```

This rule states that any file with an extension of .jpeg, .jpg, or .jpe is a JPEG file. In addition, any file that starts with the hexadecimal string <FEE7FF> (JPEG Start-Of-Image), and is followed by a character between and including 0xf0 and 0xff (JPEG APPn markers) is also a JPEG file.

An Overview of the mime.convs file

The mime.convs file contains the filters that are used to convert files from one format to another for any given MIME type. Here CUPS basically tries to construct a valid filter chain from the beginning to the end, under the directive of the PPD. Also, every filter has a virtual cost attached to it. The syntax for each rule in the file is:

```
super/type(Source) super/type(Destination) cost filter
```

- **super/type (source):** The super/type field for source is a MIME type that may use a wildcard for the super-type or sub-type (for example).

- **super/type (destination):** The destination field is a MIME type defined in the mime.types file.

- **Cost:** The cost field defines a relative cost for the filtering operation. The value for cost ranges from 1 to 100. It is used to choose between two different sets of filters when converting a file.

- **Filter:** The filter field defines the filter-program, which runs to convert the source MIME to destination MIME type. The special program "-" can be used to make the two file types equivalent. The program must accept the standard filter arguments and the environment variables described in the CUPS Interface Design Description and CUPS Software Programmers Manual.

The following are the examples of the some of the possible rules in
`mime.convs`:

```
text/plain               application/postscript   25      texttops
application/x-shell      application/postscript   25      texttops
application/vnd.cups-postscript application/vnd.cups-raster 33
pstoraster
image/* application/vnd.cups-postscript 66 imagetops
image/* application/vnd.cups-raster 33 imagetoraster
```

- In the above example, the super/type used for source are `text/plain`,
  `application/x-shell`, `image/*` and `*/postscript` and for destination
  are `application/postscript`, `application/vnd.cups-raster` and
  `application/vnd.cups-postscript`. The first two lines in the example
  use the filter `texttops` for converting plain text and x-shell application into
  generic PostScript for the cost of 25 each.

- The third line shows that the filter `pstoraster` is used to convert device-
  specific PostScript into the CUPS raster device for the cost of 33.

- In the forth and fifth line of the file the filter `imagetops` and `imagetoraster`
  are used to convert any image file into the device-specific PostScript file and
  CUPS raster for a cost of 66 and 33 respectively.

  If specified, the filename argument defines a file to read when filtering. Otherwise, the filter must read from the standard input. All filtered output must
  go to the standard output:

  ```
  program job user title options [filename]
  ```

Adding Filetypes and Filters

Adding a new file type or filter to the `mime.types` and `mime.convs` files is a
straightforward activity. However, when we upgrade to a new version of CUPS,
these files are overwritten. In such a scenario, it is better if we have created different
files with the extensions `.types` and `.convs` in the `/etc/cups` directory. This will
help you keep your configuration files intact even if CUPS is being upgraded. It is
recommended that you use the product or format name as given here. This will help
you recognize the file with its filename:

```
mycups.types
mycups.convs
```

It's not compulsory that you use the product or format name while creating these files. If you are providing a filter for a common file format or printer, you can also add the company's or even author's name:

```
acme-msword.types
acme-msword.convs
```

This helps prevent the name conflicts if you use different file types and filters. Once the names for these files are chosen, we can create them using any text editor. When these files are created and configured, we need to restart the `cupsd` process to make the changes effective.

Overview of Filter in CUPS

In `mime.convs`, many combinations can be used besides those mentioned earlier. You can also plug in your own filter. However, it needs to be compiled as per the CUPS requirements, and correct lines should be specified in the `mime.types` and `mime.convs` files.

While creating our own filter, let's assume that we have the filenames `stdin` as input and `stdout` as output. These files will use the following arguments:

- **Printer:** It defines the name of the printer queue that is normally the name of the filter being run.
- **Job:** The job ID in numeric value stands for the job being printed.
- **User:** It uses the string from the originating-user-name attribute.
- **Title:** It takes the string from the job-name attribute.
- **Copies:** It uses the numeric value from the number-copies attribute.
- **Options:** It uses the job options.
- **Filename:** This argument is optional. If we do not specify the print request file, it takes and filters data through `stdin`. In most cases, it is easy to write a simple wrapper script around the existing filters to make them work with CUPS.

An Overview of pre-filters

The PostScript in a central file format for any UNIX-based OS and it also helps CUPS generate raster data for non-PostScript printers. But if you have one of the supported file formats for non-PostScript printers, CUPS will use `prefilters` to generate output in PostScript (MIME type-application/postscript). This format doesn't include printer-specific options. So, output will be sent to the next filter, `pstops`, to add these options. Such prefilters are: `texttops`, `pdftops`, `hpgltops`.

Another prefilter that runs on all supported image formats, is the `imagetops` filter. The output of this filter is always of the MIME type `application/vnd.cups-postscript`. There is a difference between this and "application/postscript" as the `application/vnd.cups-postscript` has the print options already embedded into the file.

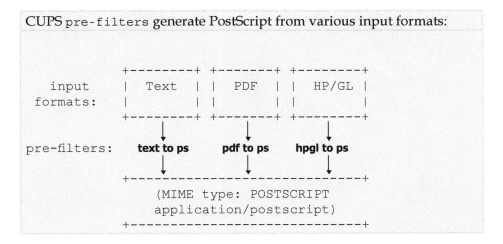

```
CUPS pre-filters generate PostScript from various input formats:


                +---------+ +--------+ +---------+
     input      |  Text   | |  PDF   | |  HP/GL  |
    formats:    |         | |        | |         |
                +---------+ +--------+ +---------+
                     |          |           |
                     v          v           v
  pre-filters:    text to ps  pdf to ps   hpgl to ps
                     |          |           |
                     v          v           v
                +----------------------------------+
                |                                  |
                   (MIME type: POSTSCRIPT
                    application/postscript)
                +----------------------------------+
```

An Overview of the pstops Filter

Initially, the MIME type of PostScript is "application/postscript". Once you have this input format, the next filter in the chain is `pstops`. Basically, the `pstops` filter converts the MIME type application/postscript to `application/vnd.cups-postscript`. Apart from the conversion, `pstops` can perform the following additional activities:

- This filter allows printing of the selected pages. For example, we can choose to print only page numbers "4, 6, 9-11, 16, and 18-21", or only odd or even-numbered pages.

- The `pstops` filter allows putting two or more logical pages on one sheet of paper. This is also called the **number-up** function.

- It counts the number of pages in the job to insert the accounting information into the `/var/log/cups/page_log`.

`pstops` counts pages, imposes multiple pages on one sheet or selects page-ranges for print:

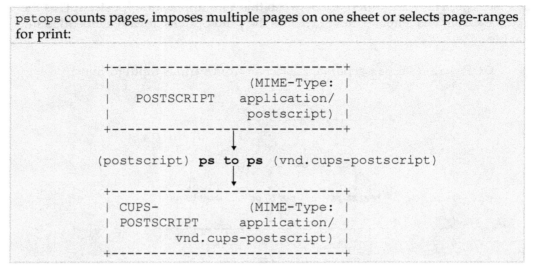

An Overview of the pstoraster Filter

The next filter is `pstoraster`, which is the core of CUPS filtering system. This filter is responsible for the rasterization process. The input is of MIME type `application/vnd.cups-postscript`, but the output is generated with the MIME type `application/vnd.cups-raster`. Please note that this output format is not yet ready to print. The files serve as a general-purpose input format for the more specialized *raster drivers* that are able to generate device-specific printer data.

`pstoraster` outputs generic raster formats, foundation for post-processing by printer-specific filters:

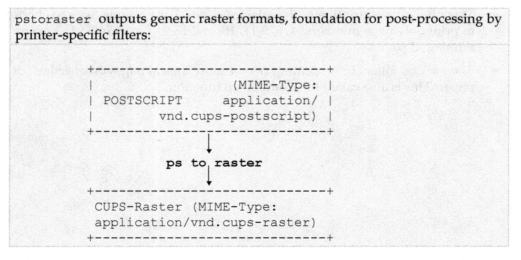

CUPS raster is a generic raster format with powerful features. It is able to include per page information, color profiles and much more, which can be used by the downstream raster drivers. The MIME type of CUPS raster is registered with IANA, and its specification is completely open.

It is designed to make it quite easy and inexpensive for manufacturers to develop Linux and UNIX raster drivers for their printer models. CUPS always takes care of the first stage of rasterization so that these vendors are freed of the GhostScript complications.

In the CUPS version prior to 1.1.15, the CUPS raster was shipped as a standalone binary filter `pstoraster`, which was derived from Ghostscript version 5.5, and could be installed separately without any conflict. But, this feature was changed and it has been integrated back into Ghostscript (GNU GhostScript 7.05).The `pstoraster` is now a simple shell script, `gs` with the parameter, `-sDEVICE=cups`. The current version of GNU Ghostscript is 8.6.

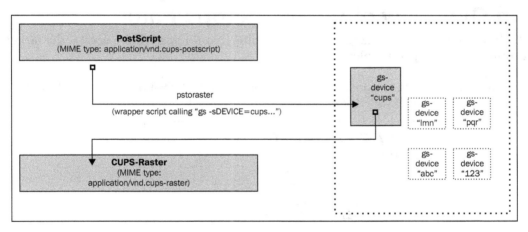

An Overview of the imagetoraster Filter

If the input file is of MIME type `image/*`, the filter `imagetoraster` will be used, which will directly convert from image to raster, without the intermediate PostScript stage. This filter plays the role of `pstoraster` for all image input files as it is the central CUPS image file RIP, used for all non-PostScript printers. The possible input MIME types are a rich variety of formats, spanning from JPEG/JFIF to PNG, GIF, TIFF, SGI-RGB, BMP, PNM (PBM/PGM/PPM), Sun-Raster, or Kodak Photo-CD, and much more.

`imgetoraster` outputs generic raster format, the foundation for post-processing by printer-.specific filters:

```
+---------------------------------------+
    (*)  JPEG/JFIF, PNG, GIF,
    (MIME-Type: SGI-RGB, TIFF, BMP,
    IMAGE(*)  image/* PNM (PBM/PGM/PPM)
+---------------------------------------+
                   |
                   v
        image  to  raster
                   |
+---------------------------------------+
    CUPS-Raster (MIME-Type:
    application/vnd.cups-raster)
+---------------------------------------+
```

An Overview of the imagetops Filter

As described in the `prefilter` section, the filter `imagetops` will be used if the target printer is PostScript-capable:

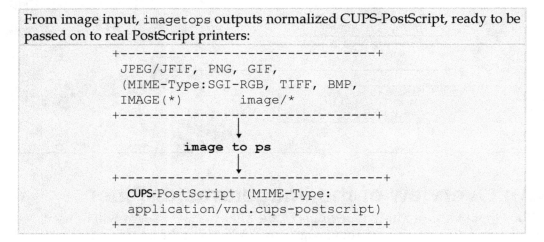

From image input, `imagetops` outputs normalized CUPS-PostScript, ready to be passed on to real PostScript printers:

```
+-----------------------------------+
    JPEG/JFIF, PNG, GIF,
    (MIME-Type:SGI-RGB, TIFF, BMP,
    IMAGE(*)        image/*
+-----------------------------------+
                 |
                 v
         image  to  ps
                 |
+-----------------------------------+
    CUPS-PostScript (MIME-Type:
    application/vnd.cups-postscript)
+-----------------------------------+
```

Rasterto and other Printer-Specific Filters

CUPS ships with a variety of raster drivers. They are used to convert the generic CUPS raster data to a printer-specific format, which embeds all the control commands to get the desired print options from the device. This is done by `rasterto` or other printer-specific filters by calling for a more general filter with printer-specific parameters.

At this point, other deliberate filters or raster drivers, which also include device-specific ones, could be bolted onto the system, for example from vendors who want to support their printers on the Linux/UNIX or Mac OS X platforms. We can see printer-specific raster drivers in the directory: `/usr/lib/cups/filter/` and thay are `rastertolabel`, `rastertohp`, `rastertoepson`, `rastertoescp`, `rastertopcl`, `rastertoturboprint`, `rastertoapdk`, `rastertodymo`, `rastertoprinter`, and so on.

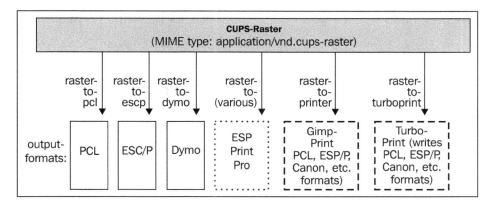

Foomatic and cupsomatic Filters

Foomatic is the database of Openprinting.org, which contains the complete information about printer models, eligible Ghostscript drivers, supported print options, and drive execution details. You can access this information online, and can also generate a current PPD for any supported printer/driver-combo, using the `PPD-O-Matic` script running on openprinting.org website.

Warning

It is not recommended to use the PPDs generated by the old script called `CUPS-O-Matic`, as they might be incompatible with some applications.

Use the following steps to generate the PPDs for any printer:

- Select the printer model
- Read related notes
- Choose the **Recommended Driver** — This is a very important choice as sometimes there may be as many as five drivers available, but always choose only the one that is recommended
- Click on **Generate PPD**
- Save the resulting PPD file and follow the instructions to install it

Besides being used with CUPS, these PPD-O-Matic-generated PPDs are also digestible for all PPD-aware programs such as StarOffice, OpenOffice, WordPerfect, or CorelDraw for Linux. The PPD contains all available information about the printer.

These PPD-aware programs can load the PPD to read stuff such as the needed page margins, the available printer fonts. They can also be used to learn which PostScript code snippet needs to go into the print file if, for example, page 7 is to be taken from paper tray 2, while page 8 needs tray 3, and the rest is from tray 4 (StarOffice).

We can also install these PPDs on any Windows client on top of an Adobe PostScript driver. The PostScript print files generated with this combo can then be sent to a CUPS server with the fitting printer installed, which will process and print the file.

For the PPD to actually work on the CUPS server, we need to have a few more preconditions met:

- You need to have the cupsomatic-Perl script installed in `/usr/lib/cups/filters/`. It mimics to be a CUPS filter, and is called from inside the PPD-O-Matic-PPD. It hands over the PostScript to an appropriate filter from your standard Ghostscript installation.
- You need to have just the mentioned Ghostscript filter installed, which is called by `cupsomatic`.
- You need to make sure some Perl modules required for `cupsomatic` to work are also installed.

The `cupsomatic` filters were perhaps the most widely used on CUPS installations. These filters utilize the traditional Ghostscript devices to deliver jobs for CUPS. Here, the whole rendering process is done in one stage inside Ghostscript, using an appropriate device for the target printer.

As we have discussed earlier, `cupsomatic` uses PPDs generated from the foomatic printer and the driver database at openprinting.org. You can recognize these PPDs from the line calling the `cupsomatic` filter.

The same approach is applied to any other non-PS-printer-PPD (like the PPD-O-Matic generated drivers) where the `mime.convs` will contain a line starting with `*cupsFilter:`

```
*cupsFilter: "application/vnd.cups-postscript  0  cupsomatic"
```

Once it has reached the MIME type, that is, device-specific PostScript `application/vnd.cups-postscript` through its standard filtering mechanism, it tells CUPS to use `cupsomatic` as the next filter. `cupsomatic` then reads the attached PPD options and constructs from them a correct Ghostscript command line to run the file through the appropriate filter. In the end, it hands over the converted file back to a CUPS backend to send it to the printer.

We can see the previously mentioned line among the first 40 lines of the PPD file. If such a PPD is installed, the printer shows up in the CUPS web interface with the name `foomatic` for the driver description.

 Cupsomatic is a Perl script that runs Ghostscript with command-line options auto constructed from the selected PPD and the command line options given to the print job. The `cupsomatic` filters are not developed by the CUPS developers and can be considered as third-party add-ons to CUPS.

Today `cupsomatic` is no longer widely used as many of the first generation PPDs that are still heavily in use do not meet the required specifications of Adobe. On the other hand, new PPDs comply these specifications and additionally they also provide a new way to specify different quality levels (hi-res photo, normal color, grayscale, and draft). Also, the download option for `cupsomatic` presents a lot of difficulties when you use them for "Point n Print" to Windows clients.

The above mentioned limitations of `cupsomatic` can be overcome if you use a better and more powerful successor currently running in late beta, which is called as `foomatic-rip`. To use `foomatic-rip` as a filter with CUPS, we need a new type of PPDs, which have a slightly different syntax:

```
*cupsFilter: "application/vnd.cups-postscript  0  foomatic-rip"
```

The PPD-generating engine at openprinting.org has now been revamped. So, the new PPDs comply with the Adobe specifications. They also provide a new way to specify different quality levels (hi-res photo, normal color, grayscale, and draft), which is the requirement for five or more different selections (media type, resolution, inktype, and dithering algorithm). There is built-in support for custom-size media. There is also support for switching print options from page to page in the middle of a job. The best thing is that the new `foomatic-rip` works seamlessly with all legacy spoolers as well (such as LPRng, BSD-LPD, PDQ, PPR, and so on), providing them access to use PPDs for their printing.

The "Point n Print" is the mechanism that is supported by Samba. In this mechanism, the clients use the printers' drivers to generate print files in the format the printer (or the UNIX print system) requires. Print files received by Samba are handed over to the CUPS, which is responsible for all further processing, as needed.

Foomatic/cupsomatic makes all working combinations of printers and Ghostscript filters available for use in CUPS.

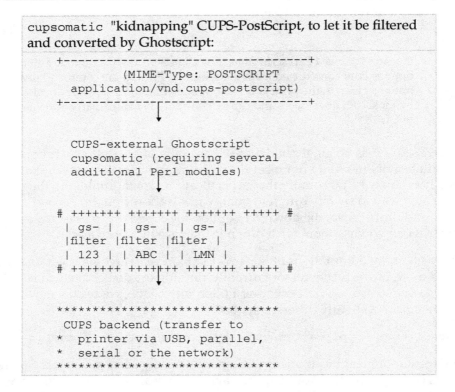

```
cupsomatic "kidnapping" CUPS-PostScript, to let it be filtered
and converted by Ghostscript:

        +-----------------------------------+
                 (MIME-Type: POSTSCRIPT
        application/vnd.cups-postscript)
        +-----------------------------------+
                          |
                          v

        CUPS-external Ghostscript
        cupsomatic (requiring several
        additional Perl modules)
                          |
                          v

    # +++++++ +++++++ +++++++ +++++ #
    | gs-  | | gs-  | | gs-  |
    |filter |filter |filter |
    | 123  | | ABC  | | LMN  |
    # +++++++ +++++++ +++++++ +++++ #
                          |
                          v

    *******************************
     CUPS backend (transfer to
    *  printer via USB, parallel,
    *  serial or the network)
    *******************************
```

Additional Filter Functionality

As we had discussed earlier, CUPS automatically constructs all possible filtering chain paths for any given MIME type, and for each installed printer. Take a scenario where there is a choice of two or more possible filtering chains for the same target printer. In such a case, how would CUPS select a particular rule?

The answer is simple. There is a cost filed in the third column of the `mime.convs` file that represents the virtual costs assigned to this filter. Every possible filtering chain will sum up to a total "filter cost". Based on that, CUPS selects the most inexpensive route.

If the value for `FilterLimit is set to 1,000` in `cupsd.conf`, `it means that it` will not allow more than 1,000 virtual filter costs to run concurrently. This is an efficient way to limit the load of any CUPS server by setting an appropriate `FilterLimit` value. A `FilterLimit` of 250 allows roughly one job at a time, while a `FilterLimit` of 1,000 allows approximately four jobs at a time.

Raw Printing

We can inform CUPS to print any file in a raw format, which means that it will not be filtered. CUPS will send the file to the printer as-is, not bothering to check if the printer would be able to digest it. In such cases, the users need to make sure that they do not send any incorrect data formats. Raw printing can happen on any queue if the `-o raw` option is specified on the command line. You can also set up raw-only queues by not associating any PPD with it.

The command is:

```
$sudo lpadmin -P cupsrawprt -v socket://10.20.30.40:9100 -E
```

The above command sets up a queue named `cupsrawprt`, which is connected via the socket protocol to the device at IP address 10.20.30.40, using port 9100. If a PPD is added with `-P /path/to/PPD` to this command line, a "normal" print queue is installed.

The Windows client systems produce printer-specific data that is often random binary data. If a "normal" print queue is set on the print server on the UNIX/Linux platform, the UNIX/Linux filtering system is not able to convert it into printer-specific data due to inherent design differences, and also because random binary data cannot be detected automatically.

If PPD is not specified with a queue, CUPS will automatically treat each job sent to a queue as "raw". However, CUPS will only send known MIME types, as defined in its own `mime.types` file, and refuse others.

Application/octet-stream Printing

If any MIME type with no rule is specified in the `/etc/cups/mime.types` file, it will be considered as unknown or `application/octet-stream`. Such files will not be sent because CUPS refuses to print unknown MIME types by default. For example, sometimes print jobs originating from Windows clients are not printed, and an error can be found in the CUPS logs: **Unable to convert file 0 to printable format for job**.

To enable the printing of application/octet-stream files, these two files have to be edited:

- `/etc/cups/mime.convs`
- `/etc/cups/mime.types`

Both these files contain entries at the end that must be uncommented to allow raw mode operation for application/octet-stream.

In `/etc/cups/mime.types`, make sure this line is present:

```
application/octet-stream
```

This line with no specific autotyping rule set makes all files, not otherwise auto-typed, a member of the application/octet-stream.

In `/etc/cups/mime.convs`, have this line:

```
application/octet-stream    application/vnd.cups-raw    0    -
```

This line tells CUPS to use the "Null Filter", which is denoted as "-" in the above example. This will not do anything on the `application/octet-stream` except that it will just only tag the result as `application/vnd.cups-raw`. The option `application/vnd.cups-raw` means a green light to the CUPS scheduler to hand over the file to the backend connecting to the printer.

Unlike traditional printing systems, CUPS is a security-aware printing system as it does not, by default, allow one to send a lot of binary data to printing devices. This could be easily abused to launch a Denial of Service attack on the printer, causing at the least, a loss of paper and ink. We will discuss CUPS DoS attack in the next chapter on *Security*.

In a Denial of Service (DoS) attack, the user sends several authentication requests to the print server, filling it up. As all requests have false return addresses, the server can't find the user when it tries to send the authentication approval. The server waits, sometimes for more than a minute, before closing the connection. When it does close the connection, the attacker sends a new batch of forged requests, and the process begins again, tying up the service indefinitely.

In CUPS, "unknown" data is designated as MIME type `application/octet-stream`. This allows us to send data "raw", for which the MIME type must be known to and allowed by CUPS.

The /etc/cups/mime.types file defines the rules as to how CUPS recognizes MIME types, whereas the /etc/cups/mime.convs file decides which file conversion filters may be applied to the MIME types. Editing the mime.convs and the mime.types file does not *enforce* "raw" printing, but only *allows* it.

PostScript Printer Descriptions (PPDs) for non-PostScript Printers

As discussed earlier, the PPDs were meant to be used for PostScript printers only that sent device-specific commands and settings to the RIP, which processed the job file. CUPS has extended this scope for PPDs to cover non-PostScript printers as well. This will make working with printers easy because PostScript is a standardized file format. CUPS handles PostScript and uses a PostScript RIP (GhostScript) to process the print job files. The only difference is that a PostScript printer has the RIP built in. For other types of printers, the GhostScript RIP runs on the host computer.

The PPDs for non-PostScript printers have a few lines that are unique to CUPS, and the most important one looks like this:

```
*cupsFilter: application/vnd.cups-raster  50    rastertoprinter
```

The above line tells the CUPS daemon to use rastertoprinter as the last filter, which serves an application/vnd.cups-raster as input in MIME type file. Therefore, CUPS should autoconstruct a filtering chain that delivers the specified MIME type as its last output.

The output is then taken as input to the specified rastertoprinter filter. After the last filter has done its work, the file should go to the backend, which sends the file to the output device.

Cupsomatic/foomatic-rip versus Native CUPS Printing

We know that the native CUPS rasterization works in two steps:

- In the first step, pstoraster uses the special CUPS device from ESP Ghostscript as its tool.
- In the second step, the rasterdriver uses various device-specific filters as there are several vendors who provide good quality filters for this step. Some of them are free software, shareware, while some are proprietary.

- This method produces better quality output and has more advantages than the other methods. `cupsomatic/foomatic-rip`.

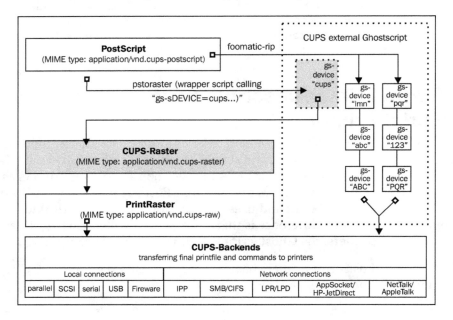

- `Foomatic-rip` is a complete rewrite of the old cupsomatic idea, but very much improved and generalized to other spoolers. An upgrade to foomatic-rip is strongly advised, especially if CUPS is also being upgraded.

- Like the old cupsomatic method, the foomatic-rip method uses the traditional Ghostscript print file processing, but does everything in a single step. Therefore, it relies on all the other devices built into Ghostscript. The quality is as good (or bad) as the Ghostscript rendering in other spoolers. The advantage is that this method supports many printer models that are yet to be supported by the more modern CUPS methods. We can use both methods side-by-side on one system and even for one printer. You only need to set up different queues and find out which one works best for you.

- The `cupsomatic` filter kidnaps the print file after the `application/vnd.cups-postscript` stage and re-routes it through the CUPS's external system-wide Ghostscript installation. Therefore, the print file bypasses the `pstoraster` filter and the CUPS raster drivers. After Ghostscript finishes its rasterization, cupsomatic hands the rendered file directly to the CUPS backend.

Examples for Filtering Chains

Let's discuss some examples of the commonly occurring filtering chains that illustrate the workings of CUPS.

Example1

Assume that we want to print a PDF file to an PostScript printer "cupsprinter". But it should print only pages 4-6, 9, 11, and 13-15, and the printing should be "two-up" and "duplex":

- Print options such as page selection as required, two-up, and duplex are passed to CUPS on the command line.

- The complete PDF file is sent to CUPS and autotyped as "application/pdf".

- The file first passes to the `pdftops` prefilter, which produces PostScript with the MIME type—"application/postscript". Please note that a preview here would still show all pages of the original PDF.

- The file then passes on to the `pstops` filter that applies the command-line options. It selects pages 4-6, 9, 11 and 13-15, creates the imposed layout of two pages on one sheet and inserts the correct duplex command into the new PostScript file as defined in the printer's PPD. The file is now assigned the PostScript MIME type, `application/vnd.cups-postscript`.

- The file goes to the socket backend, which transfers the job to the printers.

- The resulting filter chain, therefore, is as shown in the PDF to socket chain illustration.

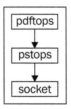

Let's assume that we want to print the same filter to a USB-connected Epson Stylus Photo printer installed with the CUPS `stphoto2.ppd` file. The first few filtering stages are nearly the same:

- Print options such as page selection as required, two-up, and duplex are passed to CUPS on the command line.

- The complete PDF file is sent to CUPS and is autotyped as "application/pdf".

- The file must first pass the `pdftops` prefilter, which assigns PostScript MIME type "application/postscript". Please note that a preview here would still show all pages of the original PDF.

- The file then passes the `pstops` filter that applies the command-line options. It selects the pages 4-6, 9, 11and 11-13, creates the imposed layout two pages on one sheet and inserts the correct duplex command into the new PostScript file. As this printer and PPD do not support duplex printing, this option will be ignored while the file is generated. This file is now assigned the PostScript MIME type — `application/vnd.cups-postscript`.

- The file then passes the `pstoraster` stage and becomes MIME type `application/cups-raster`.

- Finally, the `rastertoepson` filter does its work in the printer's PPD, creating the printer-specific raster data and embedding any user-selected print options into the print data stream.

- The file goes to the USB backend, which transfers the job to the printers.

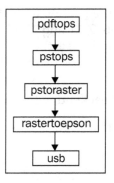

Printing with Interface Scripts

CUPS also supports use of "interface scripts", which is a known concept from the System VAT&T printing systems that works with legacy printers. These interface scripts are often used for PCL printers, and are specific to printer models that generate PCL print jobs. The functionality of these scripts is similar to PPDs for PostScript printers. These interface scripts may inject Escape sequences into the print data stream as required. This happens for example if the user selects a certain paper tray, or changes paper orientation, or uses A4 paper.

These interface scripts are rarely used in Linux, but on HP-UX platforms, they are used often. You can use any working interface script on CUPS by just installing the printer with the `-i` option:

```
$sudo lpadmin -p pclprinter -v socket://10.20.30.40:9100 \
    -i /path/to/interface-script
```

Most of us might not be aware of this script. However, with CUPS, they provide the easiest way to plug in your custom-written filtering script or program it into one specific print queue. Information about the traditional use of interface scripts can be found at:

```
http://playground.sun.com/printing/documentation/interface.html
```

An Overview of the CUPS Printing Process

The following figure shows an overview of all the filters with their relations with one another.

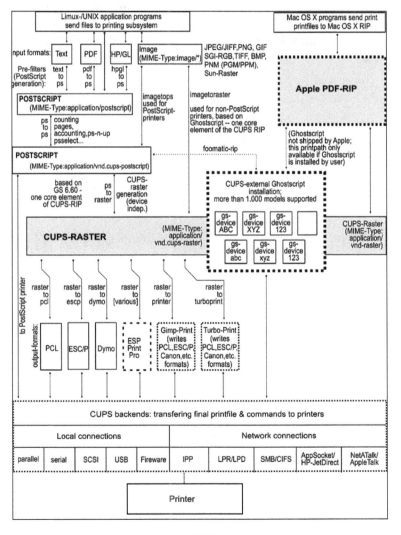

Writing your own Filter or Printer Driver

CUPS supports all file formats and filters that a printer can handle. You can write a filter, a printer driver, or a favored file format or printer if you need to. You can consult the CUPS Software Programmers Manual for step-by-step instructions.

Summary

In this chapter, we have discussed the architecture of the CUPS filtering system. It includes identifying and filtering various file formats, which helps to get print output. The CUPS filtering system has two configuration files `mime.types` and `mime.convs`, which we discussed in detail. Though CUPS can only natively understand the PostScript format, there are other filtering systems that help CUPS to work with non-PostScript printer models. In the end, we saw a detailed diagram of the CUPS printing process.

10
Security

Before starting a discussion on security in detail, let's see an overview of networking
with CUPS. CUPS as a print management system allows you to work on networking
protocol TCP/IP. You can configure any network printer or print server using the
TCP/IP protocol in CUPS. This network printer or printer server can be recognized
using the IP address, which can be configured manually, or it can be configured
automatically via network protocols such as BOOTP and DHCP.

> Bootstrap Protocol (BOOTP) is a UDP network protocol used by a
> network client to obtain its IP address automatically, while DHCP is a
> more advanced protocol that gives network information automatically
> to the clients. It can also handle BOOTP requests used to get network
> information automatically. Detailed information on this can be found at:
>
> `http://en.wikipedia.org/wiki/Dynamic_Host_`
> `Configuration_Protocol`

You can get more information on the TCP/IP functionality that CUPS supports as a
backend from the following URL:

`http://www.cups.org/documentation.php/network.html`

By default, CUPS can work as a standalone system that doesn't allow remote
connections. In such a case, CUPS will only accept print and administration requests
from a local subnet. In modern times, most CUPS installations are not being set up
on a closed network as may have been done in the past. CUPS now has to deal with
networks that are connected to the Internet, and this brings up security concerns.

Let us discuss how we can analyze the security concerns and improve the security
if a network connection is present (for sharing of printers or enabling remote
administration) in CUPS.

CUPS as a printing system provides built-in security features, which older printing systems do not provide. As discussed in Chapter 9, by default, CUPS doesn't allow binary files to be sent directly to the printer for "raw" printing. This feature is controlled in the `mime.types` file.

CUPS provides enhancements to the following security features that provide several benefits over other printing systems:

- Encryption Support
- Access Control
- Authentication Support

Encryption Support in CUPS

CUPS uses the OpenSSL, GNU TLS, and CDSA encryption libraries to provide 128-bit SSL 3.0 and TLS 1.0 encryption support for network connections.

OpenSSL is an open-source toolkit, which provides Secure Socket Layer (SSL) and Transport Layer Security (TLS) protocols, and also a general purpose cryptography library. More information can be found at: `http://openssl.org`.

The Secure Sockets Layer (SSL) protocol and its successor Transport Layer Security (TLS) are cryptographic protocols that provide secure communications on the Internet and the Intranet for various applications such as email, web browsing, printing, and so on.

GNU TLS is a project that provides security over the transport layer.

More information can be found at: `http://www.gnu.org/software/gnutls/`. Common Data Security Architecture (CDSA) is a cryptographic framework and a set of security services, which provides encryption libraries for client-server environments. More information can be found at: `http://www.opengroup.org/security/cdsa.htm`.

Configuring SSL during CUPS Installation

CUPS can integrate with OpenSSL and thus enable SSL encryption. We have already seen the steps required to configure SSL support within CUPS in Chapter 2—*Installing and Configuring CUPS*.

Encryption Support

As discussed, CUPS uses a client-server model in which the server contains the CUPS configuration files and various applications can work as clients that send print requests to the server. The print server accepts the request information and converts it into job information. CUPS supports several directives that encrypt the requests when they are sent from the client to the server. The following are such directives that can be specified in the server configuration file, `cupsd.conf`. You can specify the information on port and network address for the secure connection.

SSLListen

This directive specifies a network address and port to listen for secure connections. You can use multiple `SSLListen` directives to listen on multiple addresses and ports. This directive is similar to the `SSLPort` directive, but allows you to restrict access to specific interfaces or networks. Some examples of this directive are:

```
SSLListen 127.0.0.1:443
SSLListen 10.20.30.40:443
```

SSLPort

The `SSLPort` directive specifies a port to listen for secure connections. Here also you can specify multiple `SSLPort` lines to listen on multiple ports. Both `SSLListen` and `SSLPort` directives check `SSLListen` first, so that it can restrict the client in such way that the sever can only listen for that given port specified with the `SSLListen` directive.

An example of this directive is:

```
SSLPort 443
```

Please note that apart from dedicated HTTPS, CUPS also provides support for encryption over upgraded TLS within HTTP 1.1. In this scenario, the TLS uses an existing TCP connection. This allows unsecured and secured HTTP traffic to share the same port (in this case, http at 80 rather than https at 443). The client or server initiates an upgrade to a secure connection via some new HTTP fields and status codes. You can find more information about this "HTTP Upgrade" method in RFC 2817.

The current implementation is very basic. The CUPS client software (lp, lpr, and so on) uses encryption as requested by the server or user. The user can specify the -**E** parameter with the printing commands to force encryption of the connection.

Warning

Clients currently trust all certificates from servers. This makes the CUPS client applications vulnerable to "man-in-the middle" attacks. So, currently it is not recommended to do remote administration over WANs with existing encryption support.

A "man-in-the-middle" (MITM) attack is an active Internet attack where the attacker attempts to intercept, read, or alter information moving between two systems.

It is expected that the future versions of CUPS will have enhanced these features. It will keep track of server certificates, provide confirmation of the type of interface while accepting a new certificate, and warn about any changes made to the certificate.

The client can also specify support for encryption using the `Encryption` directive in the `client.conf` file, or in the `CUPS_ENCRYPTION` environment variable.

Encryption

The `Encryption` directive specifies the default encryption settings for the client. The following are options you can specify with this directive.

- Never — This option does not do any encryption.

  ```
  Encryption Never
  ```

- Always — This option always does SSL/TLS encryption with the help of HTTPs schemes.

  ```
  Encryption Always
  ```

- IfRequested — This option upgrades to TLS encryption if the server asks for it. This is the default setting.

  ```
  Encryption IfRequested
  ```

- Required — This option always upgrades to TLS encryption as soon as the connection is made. This is different from the `Always` mode, since the connection is initially unsecured, and the client initiates the upgrade to TLS encryption. This is very similar to using the `-E` option with the print commands.

  ```
  Encryption Required
  ```

CUPS now supports "Auto-SSL". In other words, it automatically detects when a client is connecting with SSL encryption, so it can support unencrypted, SSL-encrypted, and TLS-encrypted connections over a single port.

Access Control

CUPS supports the address-based access control mechanism. This means that when you enable remote administration, the server will use basic authentication for administration tasks. The current CUPS server supports basic, digest, and local certificate authentication. We are going to discuss each of these shortly.

Address-Based Access Control

CUPS supports address-based access control, which allows us to limit access to specific systems, networks, or domains. This method does not directly provide authentication, but allows us to limit the potential users of our system, efficiently.

As we discussed in Chapter 5—*CUPS Server Management*, CUPS maintains a list of locations that have access control and/or authentication enabled. These locations are specified using the `Location` directive:

```
<Location /cupsresrc>
  AuthClass ...
  AuthGroupName ...
  AuthType ...
  Order ...
  Allow from ...
  Deny from ...
</Location>
```

The locations generally follow the directory structure of the `DocumentRoot` directory. However, CUPS has several virtual locations for administration, classes, jobs, and printers.

Location	Description
`/admin`	This option specifies the path for all administration operations
`/classes`	This specifies the path for all classes
`/classes/cupsclass`	This option specifies the resource for class `cupsclass`
`/jobs`	This location specifies the path for all jobs
`/jobs/id`	This is the resource for job IDs
`/printers`	This specifies the path for all printers
`/printers/cupsprinter`	This path specifies the printer `cupsprinter`
`/printers/cupsprinter.ppd`	The PPD file path for printer `cupsprinter` is specified with this

Authentication Support

CUPS provides support for the both "password" and "certificate" types of authentication methods. These authentications provide ways to limit access to individuals or groups.

Authentication using Password

There are three types of password authentication, and they are:

- Basic
- Digest
- Kerberos

Let's discuss them one by one.

Basic Authentication

In basic authentication, the UNIX system's usernames and passwords are used to authenticate access to resources such as printers and classes, and to limit access to the administrative functions.

The username and password are encoded in Base64. This information is passed in plain text format from the client to the server, and hence it does not offer any protection from eavesdropping. Since in this authentication method CUPS uses the usernames and passwords of the system (UNIX/Linux or any other OS in which CUPS is configured), if any malicious user monitors network packets and discovers valid users and passwords, it could result in a serious threat to network security.

It is always recommended to use basic authentication with extreme care. You can enable encryption to hide the username and password information. Encryption is the default setting on MacOS X and on any system that has OpenSSL or GNU TLS installed.

In CUPS, implementation of basic authentication does not allow access through user accounts without a password. If one tries to authenticate using an account without a password, the access will be immediately blocked.

Once CUPS authenticates a valid username and password, any additional group membership requirements are checked.

CUPS considers anyone who is logged in as a superuser — `root`, as a member of every group.

You can use the following `AuthType` directive to enable basic authentication:

```
AuthType Basic
```

Digest Authentication

In digest authentication, usernames and passwords are defined in the `/etc/cups/passwd.md5` file to authenticate access to resources such as printers and classes, and to limit access to the administrative functions.

In basic authentication, CUPS passes the username and password strings. But in digest authentication, it passes the MD5 sum, which is basically a complicated checksum of the username and password. Moreover, digest authentication uses its own digest password file rather than the password file of the system. So even if an attacker discovers the CUPS username and password, it is less likely that the entire system will be compromised.

The current version of digest authentication in CUPS uses the client's hostname or IP address for the "nonce value". The nonce value is an additional string added to the username and password to ensure that guessing the password is made more difficult. The server checks if the nonce value matches the client's hostname or address, or rejects the MD5 sum if it doesn't. It is expected that the future versions of CUPS will support digest session authentication, which adds the request data to the MD5 sum providing even better authentication and security.

Even digest authentication does not authenticate all the inputs because it uses the client's hostname or IP address for nonce value. It doesn't guarantee that an attacker will not gain unauthorized access. However, it is safer than basic authentication and should be used instead of basic authentication whenever possible.

It is recommended that to maintain encryption, the username and password should be hidden.

 The digest authentication method is not yet supported by all web browsers.

The `lppasswd` command is used to add, change, or remove accounts from the `passwd.md5` file. The following command is used to add a user (kajol) to the default system group. You need to set the password while the user is being created:

```
$sudo lppasswd -a kajol
Password: (password)
Password again: (password)
```

Once the user is added, he or she can change his or her password using the following command:

```
$sudo lppasswd
Old password: (password)
Password: (password)
Password again: (password)
```

To remove a user from the password file, you can use the following command:

```
$sudo lppasswd -x kajol
```

Like basic authentication, here also, once a valid username and password is authenticated by CUPS, all additional group membership requirements are checked.

You can use the following `AuthType` directive to enable digest authentication:

```
AuthType Digest
```

Authentication using Certificates

Since CUPS supports certificate-based authentication, you can even use a local certificate-based authentication method. This method can be used in place of `basic` or `digest` authentication by clients connecting through the `localhost` interface.

 The local certificate authentication is not supported or allowed from clients on any other interface.

The certificate is nothing more than a 128-bit random number, which refers to an internal authentication record in the server. When a client connects to the loopback interface (localhost or `127.0.0.1` or `::1`) or domain socket, it also sends a request with an authorization header as in:

```
Authorization: Local 0123456789ABCDEFFEDCBA987643210
```

The server then looks up the local certificate and authenticates using the username associated with it. These certificates are generated by the server automatically, and are stored in the `/var/run/cups/certs` directory using the process ID of the CGI program started by the server.

These certificate files are readable only by the `User` and the `Group` defined in the `cupsd.conf` file. When the CGI program ends, the certificate is removed and invalidated automatically.

The special file `/var/run/cups/certs/0` defines the "root certificate" that can be used by any client running as the super-user, or another user who is part of the group defined by the `SystemGroup` directive. The root certificate is automatically regenerated every 5 minutes. You need to ensure that no unauthorized user is added to the system groups.

System and Group Authentication

We have already discussed the various types of authentication methods that can be specified by the `AuthType` directive. The `AuthClass` directive controls the level of authentication to be performed. `System` and `group` authentication, which extends the normal user-based authentication scheme, requires a user's membership in a system (UNIX/Linux and any other OS of CUPS) group.

To perform system authentication, each user must belong to a system group. This can be specified by the `SystemGroup` directive.

SystemGroup

This directive specifies the system administration group for both group and system authentications. The user should belong to one of the "sys", "system" or "root" groups. The actual group name depends on the operating system of the print server. These groups can be specified with the `SystemGroup` directive as follows:

```
SystemGroup sys
SystemGroup system
SystemGroup root
```

Here, the actual group depends on the operating system. For `group` authentication, each user must belong to the group specified by the `AuthGroupName` directive.

```
<Location /cupspath>
  AuthType Digest
  AuthClass Group
  AuthGroupName cupsgroup
</Location>
```

Please note that here the named group must be a valid system (UNIX/Linux or any other OS that the print server is running) user group, which is usually defined in the `/etc/group` or `/etc/netgroup` files. Also, while using digest authentication, you need to create a user account with the named group:

```
$sudo lppasswd -g cupsgroup -a kajol
```

```
Password: (password)
Password again: (password)
```

Kerberos Authentication

Kerberos is a networking protocol built on symmetric key cryptography. It requires a Trusted Third Party (TTP), which allows an individual on a non-secure network to prove their identity to one another in a secure manner. CUPS 1.3 has Kerberos support that allows you to use a Key Distribution Center (KDC) for authentication on your local CUPS server, when printing to a remote authenticated queue.

KDC is a system that distributes and manages shared and private keys for authentication of sessions on a network and access to various applications. With Kerberos, the KDC simply uses a database of all users and services in the Kerberos realm (or administrative domain). Each entry in this database is called a principal, and includes an associated encryption key. For users, this encryption key is derived from the user's password. Kerberos mostly operates symmetric encryptions done by symmetric-key algorithms.

The symmetric-key is an encryption system in which the sender and receiver of a message share a single, common key that is used to encrypt and decrypt the message. You can find more information on this encryption and algorithms from:
`http://en.wikipedia.org/wiki/Symmetric_key`

In cryptography, a Trusted Third Party (TTP) is an entity that facilitates interactions between two parties who both trust the third party. They use this mutual trust to secure their own interactions. TTPs are common in cryptographic protocols, and a very common example is a Certificate Authority (CA).

Kerberos authentication support was not available on versions older than CUPS 1.3. In order to use Kerberos-authenticated shared printers, you *must* have a version of MIT Kerberos running on the server with the `krb5_cc_new_unique()` function or *Heimdal Kerberos*. If Kerberos is installed without any of these, it will only support local Kerberos authentication.

Heimdal is an implementation of Kerberos 5. More information on this can be found at:

http://www.h51.org/

Configuring Kerberos on the System

Before configuring Kerberos with CUPS, you need to install and configure Kerberos on the system and set up a system as a KDC.

As this configuration is highly system and site-specific, it is recommended to consult the following online resources provided by the creators of Kerberos at the Massachusetts Institute of Technology (MIT).

Information related to "Kerberos: The Network Authentication Protocol" can be found at:

http://web.mit.edu/kerberos/

Mac OS X 10.2 and later supports Kerberos by default. More information about MacOS X compatibility can be checked at the following URL:

http://web.mit.edu/macdev/KfM/Common/Documentation/faq-osx.html

You can also check the Linux Documentation Project's how-to on Kerberos:

http://tldp.org/HOWTO/html_single/Kerberos-Infrastructure-HOWTO/

Configuring CUPS to use Kerberos Authentication

After the configuration of Kerberos on the system, we can then enable Kerberos authentication by selecting the "negotiate" authentication type.

The easiest way to do this is to use the following cupsctl command:

```
$sudo cupsctl DefaultAuthType=Negotiate
```

You can also enable Kerberos from the web interface by checking the **Use Kerberos Authentication** box and clicking **Change Settings**.

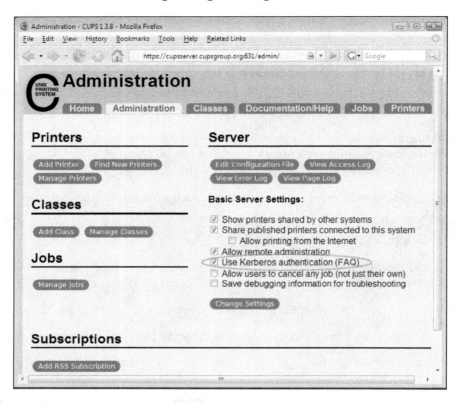

Once Kerberos authentication is enabled, you can add `AuthType Default` lines to the policies if you want to protect with Kerberos authentication. The following example shows how you can set up the policy for having Kerberos authentication for activities such as job-related operations, and printer administrative operations, printer operations, while Kerberos authentication is not enabled for any other activity.

```
<Policy mycupspolicy>
   # Job-related operations must be done by the owner or an
       administrator...
   <Limit Send-Document Send-URI Hold-Job Release-Job
      Restart-Job Purge-Jobs Set-Job-Attributes
      Create-Job-Subscription Renew-Subscription
      Cancel-Subscription Get-Notifications Reprocess-Job
```

```
Cancel-Current-Job Suspend-Current-Job Resume-Job
   CUPS-Move-Job>
   AuthType Default
   Require user @OWNER @SYSTEM
   Order deny,allow
 </Limit>
 # All administration operations require an administrator
to authenticate...
 <Limit CUPS-Add-Printer CUPS-Delete-Printer
   CUPS-Add-Class CUPS-Delete-Class CUPS-Set-Default>
   AuthType Default
   Require user @SYSTEM
   Order deny,allow
 </Limit>

 # All printer operations require a printer operator
to authenticate...
 <Limit Pause-Printer Resume-Printer
   Set-Printer-Attributes Enable-Printer Disable-Printer
   Pause-Printer-After-Current-Job Hold-New-Jobs
   Release-Held-New-Jobs Deactivate-Printer Activate-Printer
   Restart-Printer Shutdown-Printer Startup-Printer
   Promote-Job Schedule-Job-After CUPS-Accept-Jobs
   CUPS-Reject-Jobs>
   AuthType Default
   Require user varies by OS
   Order deny,allow
 </Limit>

 # Only the owner or an administrator can cancel or
authenticate a job...
 <Limit Cancel-Job CUPS-Authenticate-Job>
   Require user @OWNER @SYSTEM
   Order deny,allow
 </Limit>

 <Limit All>
   Order deny,allow
 </Limit>
</Policy>
```

CUPS implements Kerberos over HTTP using the GSS API (Generic Security Service Application Program Interface), which is a programming interface for programs to access security services. CUPS uses the ipp service for Kerberos implementation.

Currently, when only a single KDC (Key Distribution Center) is being used, delegation of credentials is needed when printing to a remote or shared printer with Kerberos authentication. So, after getting a user's Kerberos credentials, CUPS strips the @KDC portion of the username to check the group membership locally, by treating the Kerberos account as a local user account.

Now, CUPS also supports the "Authorization Services framework" on Mac OS X, which provides role-based access control in addition to the traditional UNIX model.

Protection from Denial of Service (DoS) Attacks

In this section, we will discuss some of the security risks when printer sharing or remote administration is enabled in the CUPS server. The CUPS service is vulnerable to a DoS attack, like other Internet-accessible services. CUPS will accept multiple connections to the server until it becomes overloaded and cannot process any more connections.

You can use the MaxClientsPerHost directive to control the limit for network connections from a single host. Since the MaxClientsPerHost directive is related to the directive MaxClients, we will discuss MaxClients first. Both these directives are part of the CUPS server and can be configured in cupsd.conf.

MaxClients

This directive controls the maximum number of simultaneous clients that are allowed by the server. The default value is 100 clients. The following are some examples of this directive:

```
MaxClients 100
MaxClients 512
```

Every print job requires a file descriptor for the status pipe. So while printing a large number of jobs, the CUPS server internally limits the MaxClients value to 1/3 of the available file descriptors to avoid possible problems.

MaxClientsPerHost

Like `MaxClients`, this directive also controls the maximum number of simultaneous clients allowed on a single host by the server rather than the whole server. The default value for this is the `MaxClients` value.

If its value is set to 0, then it will automatically use the `MaxClient` value. The following are some of the examples for this directive:

```
MaxClientsPerHost 0
MaxClientsPerHost 12
```

This does not prevent a distributed attack. To avoid this, we should limit access to trusted systems and networks. Here we discuss some of the possible DoS attacks with CUPS and related recommendations to protect the system:

- **Frequently open connections**

  When connections to the server are opened repeatedly and very quickly, there is no easy way to protect the server against this using the CUPS software. If the attack is coming from outside the local network, it may be possible to filter such an attack with restriction tools such as a firewall or other security application. However, once the connection request has been received by CUPS, it must accept the connection to find out who is connecting.

- **Broadcasting over single port**

  Packets are broadcast on CUPS port, for example on 631, and make the network flooded. In this case, it may be possible to disable browsing if this condition is detected by CUPS. However, if there are large numbers of printers available on the network, such an algorithm might think that an attack has occurred only when a valid update was being received.

  It is recommended that you block browse packets from foreign or distrusted networks using a router or firewall.

- **Sending partial IPP requests**

  This DoS can happen when a part of an attribute value is sent and its transmission is stopped. The current code will wait up to one second before timing out the partial value and closing the connection. This will slow the server responses to valid requests and may lead to dropped browsing packets, but will not affect the operation of the server otherwise.

  To restrict partial requests sent from foreign or distrusted networks, it is recommended that you block the IPP packets from them through a router or firewall.

- **Sending large jobs to printers**

  When very large print jobs are sent from a particular user, it indirectly prevents other users from printing. The server directive `LimitRequestBody` can be used to protect from such large print jobs.

LimitRequestBody

This directive controls the maximum size of print files, IPP requests, and HTML form data in HTTP POST requests. The default limit is 0, which disables the limit check.

The following are some examples of this directive:

```
LimitRequestBody 0
LimitRequestBody 262144
LimitRequestBody 10m
```

The directive `LimitRequestBody` limits the size of printing jobs from the user. However, this will not protect the printers from malicious users or printing files that generate hundreds or thousands of pages.

You can restrict the printer access to known hosts or networks, and can also add user-level access controls as per requirements, on expensive printers.

CUPS Release Notes

The current CUPS release notes can be found at the following URL. These notes include security fixes:

```
http://www.cups.org/relnotes.php
```

Summary

In this chapter, we have discussed the security features of CUPS including encryption and authentication methods. We have also discussed possible vectors for denial of service (DoS) attacks and how to help protect your system from them.

Index

Thank you for buying
CUPS Administrative Guide

Packt Open Source Project Royalties

When we sell a book written on an Open Source project, we pay a royalty directly to that project. Therefore by purchasing CUPS Administrative Guide, Packt will have given some of the money received to the CUPS project.

In the long term, we see ourselves and you — customers and readers of our books — as part of the Open Source ecosystem, providing sustainable revenue for the projects we publish on. Our aim at Packt is to establish publishing royalties as an essential part of the service and support a business model that sustains Open Source.

If you're working with an Open Source project that you would like us to publish on, and subsequently pay royalties to, please get in touch with us.

Writing for Packt

We welcome all inquiries from people who are interested in authoring. Book proposals should be sent to authors@packtpub.com. If your book idea is still at an early stage and you would like to discuss it first before writing a formal book proposal, contact us; one of our commissioning editors will get in touch with you.

We're not just looking for published authors; if you have strong technical skills but no writing experience, our experienced editors can help you develop a writing career, or simply get some additional reward for your expertise.

About Packt Publishing

Packt, pronounced 'packed', published its first book "Mastering phpMyAdmin for Effective MySQL Management" in April 2004 and subsequently continued to specialize in publishing highly focused books on specific technologies and solutions.

Our books and publications share the experiences of your fellow IT professionals in adapting and customizing today's systems, applications, and frameworks. Our solution-based books give you the knowledge and power to customize the software and technologies you're using to get the job done. Packt books are more specific and less general than the IT books you have seen in the past. Our unique business model allows us to bring you more focused information, giving you more of what you need to know, and less of what you don't.

Packt is a modern, yet unique publishing company, which focuses on producing quality, cutting-edge books for communities of developers, administrators, and newbies alike. For more information, please visit our website: www.PacktPub.com.

Web Host Manager Administration Guide

ISBN: 190-4-811-50-7   Paperback: 280 pages

Run your web host with the popular WebHost Manager software

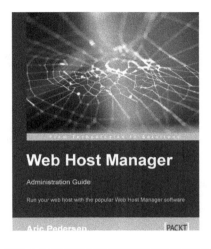

1. Set up your server using WHM's powerful server management features

2. Learn how to manage standard and reseller accounts

3. Keep an eye on your server and learn to spot problems before they become serious

cPanel User Guide and Tutorial

ISBN: 190-4-811-92-2   Paperback: 190 pages

Get the most from cPanel with this easy to follow guide

1. Everything you need to manage files, email, and databases using cPanel

2. Organise your web siteâ€¦ create subdomains, custom error messages, and password protected areas

3. Analyse site logs, ensure your site and data remain secure, and learn how to create and restore data back ups

4. Use advanced features, find powerful cPanel add ons, and install web scripts from within cPanel: osCommerce, Mambo, phpBB, and more.

Please check **www.PacktPub.com** for information on our titles